Track Cycling - Training

1st Edition

1st Edition

By Michael Mahesh
Email: **trackcyclingbook@gmail.com**

- Dedicated to Kissena Velodrome, its riders, officials and organizers over the years.

- Cover photo by Gary Berger www.garyberger.com

- Thanks to Michael Robinson for his helpful input. Thanks also to Larry & Debbie DeSario for their contributions.

Fig 1: Kissena Velodrome in the mid 80s.

Table of Contents

Preface.. 4

Chapter 1 – Types of Events........................ 11

Chapter 2 – Equipment.............................. 20

Chapter 3 – Base Line Fitness..................... 36

Chapter 4 – Energy Systems........................ 55

Chapter 5 – Training Protocols.................... 66

Chapter 6 – Weight Training........................ 90

Chapter 7 – Plyometrics.............................. 95

Chapter 8 – Weight Management................... 104

Chapter 9 – Nutrition and Supplements............. 109

Chapter 10 – Aerodynamics......................... 119

Chapter 11 – Velodrome Conditions................ 124

Chapter 12 – Road Miles............................ 127

Chapter 13 – Race Day.............................. 129

About the author...................................... 152

References and Reading List......................... 154

Glossary... 158

Index... 162

Note to the reader

There are many books and resources dedicated to the sport of Road Cycling and Triathlon racing, but none that I know of dedicated to training and racing for Track Cycling. Track Cycling is a niche / cult sport in the US and probably in other Countries; maybe that is why no one has bothered writing a book for this rather small target audience. The information in this book was gleaned over the years and comes from a variety of sources. It would certainly be great to have a comprehensive book dedicated to tactics & training for Track Cycling. Many new comers to the track have to learn by trial and error which can become quite time consuming and expensive. Track coaches are rare and costly, and only available to elite riders or those who can afford them. I hope that this book can give you some direction on how to proceed into the fast-paced world of Track Cycling.

Fig 2: 1968 Labor Day meet at Kissena – photo provided by Debbie & Larry DeSario

Preface

Track cycling – training and racing should be treated like a **project** with a definite start and a definite end. Let us say the racing season ends in October. You will then have November thru April to get ready for the track racing season, which will start in May and end in October here in New York. Training and racing involves time and cost to get yourself and equipment ready to perform to the best of your capabilities. A **training program** will therefore consist of several smaller projects and activities that all lead into getting you ready for racing. In addition, you will have a competitive edge if you can get yourself prepared in the most efficient manner without wasting time or effort. The training concept is rather simple, it entails training your energy systems and muscle memory for specific events. You would therefore have to survey your competition and see what they are doing, what times are needed to be competitive and what types of equipment would be the best value for the money. In essence, these are the steps below for the project – **Get Fit**.

Define the problem:
- **Get Fit** for track racing.

Develop solution options:
- How many different ways might you go about solving this problem and which would be the most efficient and cost effective.

Program the project:
- What must be done?
- Who will do it?
- How will it be done?
- When must it be done?
- How much will it cost?
- What is needed to do it?

Execute the program:
- The training program must now be implemented, executed and followed.

Monitor and control training progress:
- Are you on target?
- If not what must be done?
- Should the plan be changed or altered to get back on track?

Close and evaluate the project and overall program:
- What was done well?
- What should be improved?
- What else did you learn?
- What were your race results?
- Did you achieve your goals?

In summary you will want to:
- Properly plan your training.
- Define the scope of your training.
- Budget time for training.
- Budget costs for training and racing.
- Monitor the quality of training.
- Manage resources and equipment.
- Document your progress.
- Monitor your progress.
- Manage the risk of training & racing (injury & illness prevention)
- Procure the right services and equipment

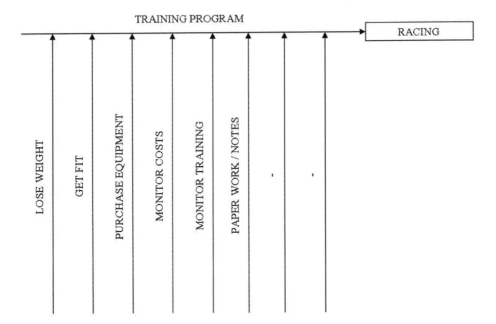

Fig 3: Basic outline of an overall training program concept consisting of various projects and activities which will go on simultaneously towards a final outcome – RACING.

Overview of Track Cycling:
Track cycling is a fast-paced, sprint type events, with several different races all performed on a velodrome, an indoor or outdoor track in the shape of an oval with large banked turns on opposing sides. Training for track cycling is different from training for other cycling events in that you are training for more anaerobic muscular endurance. Your program should be specific and your training year planned out. In addition, your program should emphasize resistance training.

Periodization is a system of training that breaks up the year into "mesocycles," or different types of training; the entire training year is separated by preparation, competition and transition times. Each mesocycle contains more specific time periods for improving each aspect of training. The idea is to build upon each aspect of fitness until you are in peak condition to perform during the competition period.

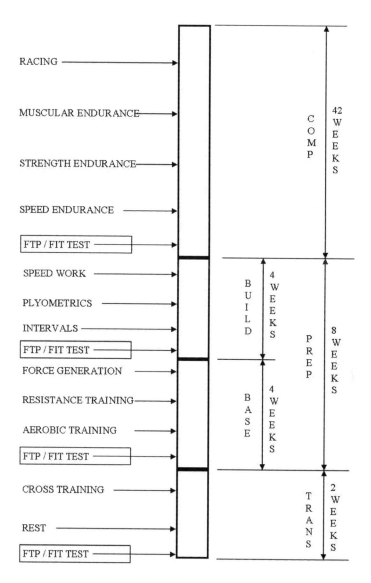

Fig 4: Basic outline of the (**Get Fit**) project as indicated above in the overall training program in Fig 3.

Preparation Base and Build Period:
The preparation period includes two weeks to prep, four weeks for a base period and four weeks for a build period. The prep period is the start of your training year, when you focus on increasing aerobic endurance with cross and resistance training. Speed skills are worked on minimally through spinning drills on an indoor trainer. The base period is used to build up a fitness base. Endurance training is cut back on, replaced by force and speed drills. Resistance training is increased and cross training is decreased. The build period begins to focus on muscular endurance and anaerobic endurance. Resistance training turns to maintenance, while more time is spent on the bike doing speed, force and power drills.

Strength Training - for a track athlete, time in the gym can mean the difference between a first or second place finish. The track athlete must have power and the ability to endure power output over a sustained period of time. The power for track cycling comes from the legs and glutes. Resistance training involving the leg press, leg extension, leg flexion, squats, deadlifts and lunges are beneficial to your training program. Resistance training is emphasized during the base period. This is where you are working hard on the bike and hard in the weight room. You begin to taper off during the preparation period, only working to maintain the muscular strength you have gained.

Plyometrics - are a type of training best fit into the build period. Plyometrics works on training the stretch-shortening cycle of muscles. This kind of training is beneficial to improving muscle force and power. Plyometric exercises are quick movements that take the muscle through its eccentric, amortization and concentric phases with speed and force. Plyometric exercises for a track cyclist include the squat jump, split squat jump and the single-leg vertical jump. Plyometrics can be combined with resistance training through a complex-training program. The schedule of a complex-training program involves high-intensity resistance training followed by plyometric exercises. If you are doing a complex-training program, allow a minimum of 48 hours of rest between complex training sessions.

Competition Period

The competition period is split into peak and race weeks. During the peak period, training volume is reduced, but intensity is increased. Training like you are racing is ideal during this time. The race period emphasizes muscular endurance and strength. Races provide most of the fitness you need. During off weeks, work on emphasizing strength, power and speed. Also do some early season road races and criteriums for fun – it's not a job.

Transition Period

The transition period comes after your racing season has ended. This is a time to rest and recover from the hard year of training. There is generally little to no schedule during transition periods. It is a time to ride for pure enjoyment and allow your body to rest. If you are the kind of track athlete who likes to participate in other cycling races, such as cyclocross, which begins just as the track season is ending, your transition period may be short. Just be sure to keep well rested between racing seasons.

Summary:
Preparation base and build period:
- Aerobic endurance
- Resistance training / strength training
- Force
- Speed
- Plyometrics

Competition period:
- Racing
- Muscular Endurance
- Strength Maintenance
- Speed Endurance

Transition Period:

- Cross training
- Time off

Why do we train:
We train to be prepared for the highest level of performance possible through physical development, sport specific development, technical skills, tactical abilities, psychological factors, injury resistance and theoretical knowledge. We train so that our bodies and minds can adapt and improve to the specific needs of our sport. There is rapid initial improvement during the preparatory phase and then we plateau during the competitive phase. The training program then has to be modified to prevent burn out or stagnation. Therefore when we train there is an immediate training effect, a delayed training effect and a cumulative training effect as time goes by. Also activities that fire up the dopamine system in our bodies and push us to learn new skills can be very rewarding. A hard workout releases endorphins which are the feel good hormones that give you a feeling of accomplishment. In other words being active keeps you healthy and keeps the negative hormones at bay such as cortisol. Some athletes may even suffer mild Post Traumatic Syndrome Disorder (PTSD) when they stop training and competing, since the adrenalin rush of competition can be quite addictive and stress reducing. One must also be cautious to not suffer burn out when taking part in sports, it can quickly become time consuming and all encompassing. Your part time sport should not become your full time job, after all you are only an amateur and you are not getting paid to take part in your sport. There should be a balance in everything you do.

Chapter 1 – Types of Events

Olympic Events

Sprints

The sprints are probably the most well known track event. Based on the rider's time during a 200-meter time trial (see below), he or she is seeded into a bracket and tries to advance through several rounds of racing to the final. Each race is three laps on a 250 meter or smaller track or 2 laps on a 333 meter or larger track, and is generally contested between two or three riders. The first rider across the finish line wins. Riders generally do not go all out for the entire race; riders most often employ cat-and-mouse tactics to gain an edge in the final sprint to the finish line. The race is very short, fast and explosive.

Tip: Know your competitor's strengths and weaknesses and keep an eye on them at all times.

Keirins

Six riders draw lots to determine their start position. The first person to cross the finish line after two kilometers wins. The riders are paced behind a Derny (a motorized bicycle), which gradually accelerates up to 50 kilometers per hour (about 30 mph) before it pulls off the track approximately 600 meters from the finish line. Riders jockey for position behind the Derny, trying to position themselves well for the sprint to the finish. The event is wildly popular in Japan, where betting on racers is permitted.

Tip: The race is often an aggressive, physical race, so prepare to defend your position.

Fig 5: A rider training at Kissena

Team Sprint

The team sprint, or Olympic sprint as it is sometimes called, is a 3-lap timed race between teams of three racers. The winner is the team with the fastest time. The riders making up a team, line up side-by-side on the start line and begin the race from a standing start with holders and then form into a pace line after the start. The first rider sets the pace for one lap and then peels off and out of the race. The remaining riders continue on, with the second rider taking his turn in front. After completing a lap, the second rider pulls up and out of the way of the final rider who completes the third lap alone. Two teams race on the track at the same time, starting on opposite sides of the track. Originally just contested by men, the team sprint is now also a women's event. The women's event is two laps, contested by two athletes.

Tip: The order in which the riders start is very important to the success of the team. Faster rider should start first and endurance rider should be last.

Fig 6: Riders doing a sprint at Kissena – photo by Gary Berger.

Team Pursuit

The team pursuit is a timed event where teams of four riders race for 4 kilometers. The team with the fastest time wins. Teams are seeded based on a qualifying round and then compete in rounds to reach the final. As in the team sprint, the riders start from a standing start and then take advantage of drafting by filing in line behind each other. They take turns riding at the front and pull off in the turns, using the banking of the track to help them drop back in at the end of the line. Usually riders take half lap or one lap "pulls" at the front of the pack. Two teams race on the track at the same time, starting on opposite sides of the track. If one team overtakes the other team, they automatically advance, unless it is in the qualifying round where time is the only important factor. Originally just contested by men, it is now also a women's event. The women's event is 3 kilometers and contested by three athletes.

Tip: Don't overlap wheels!

Omnium
The omnium is multi-race event. The rider with the best overall performance in all the events based on points, is the winner. The event is best suited to an all-around athlete, one who has speed and endurance.

Individual Pursuit
Like the team pursuit, the individual pursuit is a timed event which begins from a standing start. The rider with the fastest time wins. Riders are seeded in brackets based on a qualifying round and then compete in rounds to determine the winner. Two riders race on the track at the same time, starting on opposite sides of the track. If one rider overtakes the other rider, they automatically advance, unless it is in the qualifying round where time is the only important factor. As part of the omnium, the individual pursuit is contested over three kilometers, but, historically, the men covered four kilometers and the women three kilometers.

Tip: Learning to pace yourself and trying to ride specific lap times is key.

200-Meter Sprint Time Trial

This is historically not a stand-alone race, but is used for time trials to seed racers for the sprint race. From a rolling start, individual riders do a time trial where they wind up their selected gear to build speed to see who can cover 200 meters in the fastest time. Riders get a couple of laps to build up speed and then dive down the banking to pick up speed.

Tip: The white line is the shortest and fastest distance around the track, so stick to it. (*You can't, at high speeds over 33 mph stick to the white line at Kissena's 400 meter track, especially in gears over 90". If you do try, you will be thrown wide in turn four, since the track has shallow bankings. The fastest path at Kissena is to stay close to the red line.*)

One Kilometer Time Trial – 1000 meters

The Kilo, as it is often referred, is a time trial begun from a standing start. The rider who completes the distance with the fastest time wins. There are no rounds or second chances, it is a one-time effort and the fastest rider on that day wins.

Tip: On the second lap it helps to float, just a little bit, so you can have a strong last lap.

Points Race

Traditionally a much longer race, the points race combines both endurance and speed. The first four riders across the line on sprint or point laps are awarded points (five points for first, three for second, two for third and one for fourth). Any rider who laps the field receives 20 points. The rider with the most points wins. This is a very tactical event; depending on their strengths, some riders rely on their endurance and attempt to earn points by gaining laps and others rely on their sprinting ability to gain points by finishing first at the ten lap marks.

Tip: Try to keep track of how many points you have as well as your competition. (*I usually try to keep track of which lap I am*

*going to get dropped. I find it is quite hard to do math in the
anaerobic range, but then again I have nothing to add 0+0 =0
points, the only number I can recognize is 195.....which is my
pulse just before I get dropped like a rock. I am not a points
racer, I am more of Kilo, Sprint and Scratch rider.)*

Scratch Race
Scratch races are one of the more straightforward track races.
While the Olympic event is 5 kilometers, scratch races can be
any length. The event is a mass start event, meaning a lot of
riders race at the same time. The first rider to cross the finish line
wins.

Tip: Positioning is very important: in most cases it is best to stay
up near the front of the group so you can react to moves by your
competition.

Other Track Events

Madison
Internationally, the Madison was traditionally a 50-kilometer
race, which is two hundred laps on a 250 meter track. It is set up
a lot like a points race, but, instead of sprinting every 10 laps,
riders sprint every 20 laps. The first four riders across the line at
the 20 lap intervals are awarded points for their team for each
sprint (five points for first place, three for second, two for third
and one for fourth). Riders race in two-person teams. The
teammates take turns actively racing. The rider not actively
racing "rests" by riding higher up on the track waiting to go back
into the race. The riders exchange places by using their hands to
sling each other into the race. The team with the most points at
the end of the race wins.

Tip: Keep your head up, there is a lot going on and you don't
want to run into the back of another team that is in the middle of
exchanging positions.

Miss and Out

The length of a miss and out is determined by the number of riders in the race. Every lap the last rider across the finish line is eliminated from the race, until only one rider remains. In some cases, riders are eliminated until three remain, and then the remaining three riders race one more lap, with the first rider across the line winning. The most important part of this race is your positioning on the track compared to the rest of the riders.

Tip: The back of the pack, near the bottom of the track, is the worst place to be. Riders surge over the top at the last minute leaving you exposed.

Win and Out

In the Win and Out, the first person across the line on the lap determined by the officials as a bell lap, wins and pulls out the race. The race continues, and the first person across the line on the next bell lap takes second and pulls out. This continues for a set number of laps, often with the last lap being a sprint for the remaining places.

Tip: Get a good start! *(At Kissena the win and out lap is every three laps - first sprint occurs after three laps, second sprint after 6 laps and final sprint after 9 laps. You are therefore looking at a nine lap race. It would be interesting if there was a sprint on the first three consecutive laps.)*

Point a Lap/ Snowball

The point a lap race is pre-determined number of laps. On the first lap, 1 point is awarded to the first rider across the line, the second lap 2 points are awarded, and so on. Riders have to decide their strategy; whether to go for points early, later, or sporadically throughout the race.

Tip: Decide what your strategy will be before you start, but take the opportunities that present themselves.

Unknown Distance

In the Unknown Distance race, officials determine ahead of time what the length of the race will be, but they don't tell the riders. Riders begin racing not knowing whether the race will be 1 lap or 20. The officials signal one lap to go by ringing a bell. The rider who crosses the finish line first on the final lap wins.

Tip: It helps if you're psychic. (Most of the time they aren't very long races.)

500-Meter Time Trial

The 500-meter individual time trial is a race against the clock. It begins from a standing start. The rider who covers the distance in the shortest amount of time wins. There are no rounds or chances; it is a one-time effort and the fastest rider on that day wins.

Tip: Go all out from the start in the right gear.

Chariot Race

Riders line up at the start and finish line with holders, riders are given a strong push by the holders when the whistle blows for the start. Rider who crosses the line first is the winner for this one lap race. If there are too many riders to run one race, then multiple heats will take place where the top 1 to 3 riders will qualify for the finals.

Tip: Get either a wrestler, football or rugby player to push you, then ride fast.

750-Meter Time Trial

The 750-meter individual time trial is a race against the clock for masters instead of them riding a full Kilometer time trial.

Fig 7: Riders lining up for a Chariot race at Kissena

Fig 8: 1982 Labor Day meet at Kissena – photo provided by
Debbie & Larry DeSario

Chapter 2 – Equipment

It is a given things will change - bicycle technology is progressing almost as rapidly as computer technology. Who would have thought we were going to have carbon fiber bicycles and components outfitted with Garmin GPS / Power meter devices, electronic shifting has already hit the market. It was only 20 years ago, a bicycle made with alloy Columbus SL tubing and outfitted with Campy parts and a heart rate monitor was considered cutting edge. All I can remember of my track bike from the 80s was that it was a Riggio. I can't remember what the components were nor the gearing I used – I didn't see the value of keeping notes back then. The Riggio was an upgrade from a cheap Lotus track bike, which was more of a fixed gear bike for the road. There are many options out there for buying a track bicycle. The most important thing is that the bike fits you properly and not the weight of the bicycle.

Fig 9: 2004 Reopening of Kissena - Keirin event.

I made the mistake of buying an off the shelf Bianchi Pista Concept that was one size too small for me, the next size up would have been too large. A custom made bicycle frame is probably the best way to go, unless you can get a frame that matches your body geometry. Also your body geometry might not be in proportion or symmetrical, one leg might be longer than the other, or you might have long arms as compared to the rest of your body. Forget about that rule of thumb where you track bicycle should be smaller than your road bike, that simply does not make sense. Below is the cost and component breakdown of a custom Tiemeyer track bicycle that was built for me in 2009. The Affinity Bicycle Store in New York has a similar custom made track bicycle called the 'Affinity Kissena' which is great value for the money in a custom frame. It is also a given that we would be subjected to marketing hype and equipment promoted by athletes with influence.

Fig 10: A rider riding the 'Affinity Kissena' Track Frame.

The economics of the sport is to sell the unsuspecting customer very expensive equipment. The unsuspecting customer who will think that $3,000 dollars on a set of wheels will tremendously improve their performance, also the dopamine system is fired up when we go shopping and we believe the next purchase will dramatically change our lives or performance. Marketing and advertising plays on these emotional responses, where shopping releases endorphins, buying equipment for your hobbies releases endorphins and helps your immune system just as a hard training session does.

2009 Costs:
Frame – Tiemeyer Standard Signature Aluminium Frame with headset & fork ($1,350)
(A very well designed aerodynamic and stiff frame. This is not a plug for Tiemeyer, he is no longer in business. But his attention to details was excellent - such as the titanium dropouts which prevent grooving from wheel bolts, also the dropouts are extra long to accommodate a wide variety of gear ratios without having to change the chain.)

- **Headset – Chris King**
  (Recommended by David Tiemeyer)

- **Fork – Reynolds Track Carbon Fiber**
  (Recommended by David Tiemeyer)

- **Seat post – Thompson seat post ($90)**
  (Recommended by David Tiemeyer)

- **Seat – Selle Italia ($50)**
  (Comfortable saddle)

- **Stem – Thompson 90mm ($90)**
  (Recommended by David Tiemeyer)

- **Handlebars – Deda Pista Track Bars 42cm ($100)**
  (Seems to be a popular aluminum bar)

- **Bottom Bracket – Campagnolo Record Track (68x111, English) Sealed ($150)**
  (Recommended by David Tiemeyer)

- **Crank – Sugino Grand Mighty 170mm ($290)**
  (This crank is a step up from the Sugino 75. Chain rings are easy to change since nuts are part of the crank - you don't have to worry about holding them in place when removing bolts. This makes for a more pleasant experience when changing gear ratios.) Crank arm length is of importance based on your body geometry and the events you are taking part in.

- **Chain – Izumi V NJS Approved Track Chain ($80)**
  (This is a robust chain designed for Keirin racing, consisting of a screw type master link. You do have to keep an eye on the screw type master link connection to make sure it is tight, vibrations tend to loosen the connection when the chain is new.)

- **Wheels – Mavic Ellipse Clinchers ($500)**
  (These are bomb proof wheels, had them for five years now and never had to true nor do anything to them except change tires. Used for training, sprinting and racing)

- **Tires – Vittoria Open Corsa Evo CX 23mm Clinchers for Mavic Ellipse. ($60 each)**
  (Great supple lightweight clincher tires. I've notice that 125 psi is the optimum pressure for these tires on Kissena Track.)

- **Wheels – Karbona Disk & Tri Spoke Tubular ($1,000 for pair)**
  (Value for the money carbon fiber wheels ordered directly from Taiwan. These are used for time trials and racing.)

- **Tires – Tufo S3 Lite Tubular 19mm Front & 21mm Rear ($60 each)**
  (Lightweight high pressure tubular with 19mm tubular on the front for better aerodynamics on the Karbona carbon fiber tri spoke wheel and 21mm on the disk. I've noticed that 140 psi with these tires seem to be the optimum pressure for Kissena track, anything higher and you are in for a rough bumpy ride especially when using aero bars.)

- **Chainrings – Sugino & FSA ($50 each)**
  (These are the most popular and affordable brands. Chain rings in my set are 47, 48, 49, 50, 51, 52 & 53)

- **Cogs – Dura Ace ($20)**
  (Most widely available and popular. Cogs in my set 12, 13, 14, 15, 16. Gear ratios which I use are 79 to 86 for warm up and 88, 90, 92 & 94 for racing, 96 to 108 for time trials)

- **Shoes – Specialized Body Geometry Pro Road Shoe ($250)**
  (Specialized body geometry products are well designed and best value for the money without breaking the bank.)

- **Pedals – Shimano DurAce SPD - SL 7810 ($250)**
  (I've pulled out one too many times from the Nashbar Look styled $40 pedals on the track. It is a shame the weakest link on my track bike set up were the Nashbar Look pedals, using 'no float' black cleats. The only reason for using these pedals was to be able to use the same shoe on my road bike, spin bike and track bike. I therefore needed a better solution for the track. I got the Shimano SPD style pedals and added a toe strap at the back using tie wraps. This solution is more secure with the no float cleats - the tension on these pedals are very high, the toe straps are an added security measure for

standing starts. There is no way of simply adding a toe strap to the Nashbar Look styled pedals.)

There is something unique and special about a Tiemeyer bicycle frame, which I nick named the Copter Bike, since its bladed tubes resemble a helicopter's rotor airfoils. David Tiemeyer was an engineer working on helicopters, so it is no coincidence some of his experience translated into designing fast bicycles. After doing some research and reading a few reports I decided to contact David Tiemeyer on purchasing one of his track frames. The process was easy with David paying attention to every little detail.

Fig 11: Tiemeyer track frames at Kissena

Step 1:
The sizing calculator on Tiemeyer's website allows you to input critical body dimensions and then it outputs what your frame dimensions should be depending on the events you want to specialize. David took these dimensions and the measurements from my current track frame and overlaid them onto one of his

25

standard track frames. The dimensions matched perfectly to one of his larger Signature Series track frames which was suited for all round track events, but optimized for the sprint events with the overlay fit dimensions.

Step 2:
David then sent me a link to the spectrum paint website to select a color which the frame should be painted. I selected a color and frame was painted and shipped to me in a couple of weeks after placing the order. The frame arrived with a Chris King headset, Reynolds carbon fork, warranty and a drawing with critical dimensions showing seat height, stem length and other important dimensions for fitting the bike.

Step 3:
Assembling the bike was done at the local bike shop. David recommended a Campy sealed bottom bracket for my Sugino Grand Mighty Crank. Other components which I selected were a Thomson stem, Deda Pista bars, Keirin heavy duty chain, Selle Italia seat and my existing Mavic Ellipse wheels.

Step 4:
It was now time for a test ride, after bike assembly and dialing in the positions as laid out in David's drawing. I headed for the track but there was snow on the track. I ended up doing a few laps around the flag pole to get a feel for the bike. It looked like a thoroughbred and felt like one, even though I was not able to take it for a full test on the track. My initial perception - the bike felt rigid and very stiff.

Step 5:
High speed tests on Kissena track confirmed my initial perception of the rigidity and stiffness of the frame. This was further reinforced by feeling every single bump on Kissena track which at some points could double as a washing board. This bike does not absorb the bumps, which means it would also transfer your pedal power to the wheels without any loss – for every action there is an equal and opposite reaction. The frame is

slightly heavier than normal, but this does not matter on the track and would certainly add to the rigidity of the bike's rocket feel. I feel very comfortable on the bike; it handles well during my motor pacing sessions. It has also handled well during the racing seasons and it is a great all round bicycle.

This is the configuration of my Tiemeyer bicycle:

- Chris King headset
- Reynolds fork
- Campy sealed bottom bracket
- Sugino Grand Mighty 170mm cranks
- FSA chain rings
- Dura Ace cogs
- Heavy duty keirin chain
- Thompson 90 mm stem
- Deda 42cm aluminum track bars
- Selle Italia titanium saddle
- Thompson seat post.
- Mavic Ellipse clinchers with Vittoria open corsa tires
- Shimano Dura Ace pedals with supplemental toe straps.

Track Gearing
The biggest difference between track and road racing is the attitude towards the use of gears. Gearing on the road isn't thought about all that much, except perhaps for juniors who have to comply with gear restrictions. At any given time, riders commonly don't know what gear they are in. By contrast, on the track, gears are a precise matter, and gears are chosen very specifically for each event.

As an opening note, track racers talk in gear inches – not teeth. Track racers invariably use much smaller gears (and therefore, pedal at much higher cadences) than their peers on the road.

The real difference between road and track racing is best understood when you realize that track racers don't just provide short bursts at 140 rpms. Because elite track races commonly proceed at 50 – 55 kph (31 – 34 mph) for long periods, track racers sustain 120 – 130 rpms throughout much of the race, and then accelerate to over 140 rpms for the sprints. Hitting 140 rpm's for a sprint isn't hard – any roadie can do that. Sustaining 120 to 130 rpm's for an entire race (no freewheeling!) and then hitting 140 rpm's in the sprint is hard for most roadies – it takes some training.

So when they start out on the track, many experienced roadies just figure that the track racers must have it wrong, and choose an enormous gear (say, a 51 x 14 – 98.4"). That's what I did. It doesn't work for mass start track races.

So, why do track racers use such small gears? If you're going into a race with only one gear, you are going to optimize that gear to the most critical moments in the race. But the most critical moments in a race aren't just the sprints; they are the accelerations, too. The problem with riding a relatively large gear on the track is that it accelerates more slowly (a distinct disadvantage when you need to jump hard to stay near the front), and ramping that gear up for repeated accelerations will burn your legs out over the course of a race.

So you want a gear that can do two things: efficiently get you through repeated accelerations. In a typical 92" gear (48 x 14), when the field is proceeding along at 40 kph (25 mph), you will be turning about 91 rpms. When there is an acceleration up to 50 kph (31 mph), you will need to produce 114 rpms. To accelerate again up to 60 kph (37 mph), you will hit about 137 rpms. Other factors for selecting small gears may include the fact that there is no freewheeling – so track racers never get to rest their legs altogether between major efforts.

So, what does track gearing look like in practice? The table below shows a typical selection of chainrings and cogs that a track racer would keep in stock, and the gear inches they produce with a 700 x 23 tire, rounded to the nearest half-inch.

	12	13	14	15	16	17	18
57	128.3	118.4	110.0	102.6	96.2	90.5	85.5
56	126.0	116.3	108.0	100.8	94.5	89.0	84.0
55	123.8	114.3	106.1	99.0	92.8	87.4	82.5
54	121.5	112.2	104.2	97.2	91.1	85.8	81.0
53	119.3	110.1	102.2	95.4	89.5	84.2	79.5
52	117.0	108.0	100.3	93.6	87.8	82.6	78.0
51	114.8	105.9	98.4	91.8	86.1	81.0	76.5
50	112.5	103.9	96.4	90.0	84.4	79.4	75.0
49	110.3	101.8	94.5	88.2	82.7	77.8	73.5
48	108.0	99.7	92.6	86.4	81.0	76.3	72.0
47	105.8	97.6	90.7	84.6	79.3	74.7	70.5
46	103.5	95.6	88.7	82.8	77.6	73.1	69.0
45	101.3	93.5	86.8	81.0	76.0	71.5	67.5
44	99.0	91.4	84.9	79.2	74.3	69.9	66.0
43	96.8	89.3	82.9	77.4	72.6	68.3	64.5
42	94.5	87.2	81.0	75.6	70.9	66.7	63.0

Fig 12: A sample gear chart showing various gear combinations in shaded rectangle used for training and racing.

There is a great app for the iPhone called Bike Gears that helps you see what different gears and wheel combinations will give you in terms of RPMs and speed. It must be noted that bigger gears and crank arm lengths are being used these days and times are getting faster on the track as a result of better aerodynamics of equipment. Also a lot of aerospace engineers gravitated towards the bicycle industry when there was a down turn in the aerospace industry. This resulted in better materials such as carbon fiber being used to produce equipment, better testing and better designs. It must also be noted that the Wright Brothers who were responsible for building one of the first flying aircrafts in North America were bicycle mechanics. So it seems there is a lot of cross over between flying and cycling in terms of mechanical and aerodynamic aspects.

Aero Bars

Aero bars are supposed to make you go faster by reducing frontal area whereby reducing aerodynamic drag, especially when speeds reach 30 mph. I therefore bought a Vision Tech aero bar with integrated stem, elbow rest and straight extensions, nothing could be adjusted, everything was fixed in place on this bar. The only adjustment you could make was raising or lowering the elbow rests. This was of no help since it was more important to be able to space the elbow rests apart. Surprisingly I did slower kilo times with this aero bar on several occasions than I did with my conventional track bar, it was puzzling. I just spent $275 dollars for a bar which made me go slower. Could it be the elbow rests were too close to the stem making it difficult to control the bike at speed? Could it be I was not able to leverage my upper body because the extensions placed my hands in a downward position which did not give me anything to resist or pull against without making the front wheel unstable?

I decided to ditch the Vision Tech aero bars and use the conventional track bars to do my subsequent kilos. This particular Vision Tech bar might be more suited for a road time trial which is not as violent as the track kilo. This bar did not allow for you to use brute force and leverage, it was more for finesse.

Fig 13: A rider training at Kissena in aero bars

Recently I revisited the idea of using an aero bar. I bought a different one - a Profile for $90 which had lateral adjustable elbow rests and upward curving extensions. I found this bar worked perfectly once the elbow rests were adjusted wide enough to provide optimal steering but still maintaining aerodynamic benefits. I needed the elbow rests spaced wide enough apart to provide control since Kissena track is very bumpy and it is difficult to control the bike with an aero bar when going over 25 mph. The upward curving extensions also allowed me to leverage more upper body and core strength into the pedal stroke, especially in the final half lap of the kilo when your legs are on fire.

I have finally found an aero bar which serves my personal preferences and riding style. The experimentation, trial and error is what makes cycling such an expensive sport. You need to wade through all the hype to see what works for you. Also, more expensive does not necessarily mean better performance. Dartfish has a nice little App for the iPhone or the Android devices called **Dartfish Express** which helps you analyze your position on the bicycle using photos.

Also before you get carried away with buying expensive aero equipment, you first have to look at yourself and fitness levels. There is no point in buying aero equipment when you are carrying around excess weight, you first need to lose that fat and get your body in a fit and aerodynamic state before spending dollars on aero equipment. After all your body is responsible for about 60% of the drag encountered on the bicycle. Some aero equipment below are:

- Disk wheels
- Aero helmets
- Aero handlebars
- Deep rim carbon fiber wheels.
- Long sleeve skinsuits
- Short sleeve skinsuits
- Full fingered gloves
- Shoe covers

These items can run into the thousands of dollars, it all comes down to affordability, utility, return on investment and value for the money.

Fig 14: The Saris Cyclops 300PT spin bike.

The best piece of cycling equipment I ever bought that meets the criteria of utility, return on investment and value for the money was a Cyclops 300PT spin bicycle with power meter and heart rate functions for $2,000. This allowed me to train indoors and simulate track efforts at my convenience regardless of weather or time of year, and it allowed me to measure and quantify my training and progress. I have gotten the most utility and return on investment from this piece of equipment out of all of my cycling equipment.

Below are some examples of track equipment that will give you sticker shock:

Fig 15: Giro Attack helmet - $250

Fig 16: 3T handlebars - $400

Fig 17: Mavic Comete rear disk wheel - $3,000

Fig 18: Mavic IO front wheel - $4,000

Chapter 3 – Base Line Fitness:

Components of Physical Fitness:

Health Related components: Those factors that are related to how well the systems of your body work

1. Cardiovascular Fitness: The ability of the circulatory system (heart and blood vessels) to supply oxygen to working muscles during exercise.

2. Body Composition: The relative percentage of body fat compared to lean body mass (muscle, bone, water,etc)

3. Flexibility: The range of movement possible at various joints.

4. Muscular strength: The amount of force that can be produced by a single contraction of a muscle

5. Muscular endurance: The ability of a muscle group to continue muscle movement over a length of time.

Fig 19: 2004 reopening of Kissena - Scratch race

Skill Related Components: Those aspects of fitness which form the basis for successful sports participation.

1. Speed: The ability to move quickly from one point to another

2. Agility: The ability of the body to change direction quickly

3. Balance: The ability to maintain an upright posture while still or moving

4. Coordination: Integration with hand and/or foot movements with the input of the senses.

5. Reaction Time: Amount of time it takes to get moving.

6. Power: The ability to do strength work at an explosive pace.

Components required for Cycling:

1. Endurance: The ability to continue a ride at an aerobic effort level without the onset of undue fatigue. This is specific to an event, and is the most basic and important ability.

2. Speed Skills: The ability to move the pedals quickly and efficiently, while being totally relaxed.

3. Force or strength: The ability to overcome resistance as in climbing short steep hills or turning a bigger gear, or riding into a head wind.

4. Muscular Endurance: The ability to sustain a high muscular effort for a sustained or prolonged period of time, as in a time trial. This is a combination of force and endurance.

5. Anaerobic Endurance: The ability to resist fatigue while turning a high cadence in a bigger gear. A combination of speed and endurance or speed endurance.

6. Power: The ability to apply maximum force in the shortest time possible. A combination of force and speed gives you power such as in a standing start.

Cycling training varies greatly across the disciplines. From the intense, anaerobically demanding speedway events to the ultra-endurance stage races, each cycling discipline requires a different training approach. Even within the same discipline, variations in distance will have a significant effect on a cyclist fitness regime. Professional road cyclists posses exceptional endurance. While VO2max is not always a good predictor of performance in elite endurance athletes, studies have shown that aerobic power is high in this group of performers. More accurate predictors of performance include lactate threshold, maximal lactate steady state and power output at lactate threshold. Lactate threshold has been shown to be as high as 90% of VO2max in professional cyclists.

Peak power output can also be used to predict cycling performance across the disciplines. For competitive road cyclists, anaerobic power is required for the mass start, hill climbing and a sprint finish. It may be even more important for off-road cyclists and is obviously a prerequisite for track racing. Traditionally, cycling coaches have prescribed increases in training volume to induce overload and adaptation. Yet it may be that a reduction in volume and integration of interval sprint training may be more beneficial. Not only has this shown to improve peak power output and capacity, it also increases VO2max to a greater extent compared to lower intensity, longer duration training.

Interval Training for Sport-Specific Endurance - Distance cyclists have traditionally favored long, slow distance training almost to the exclusion of all else. But substituting a small percentage of weekly mileage for shorter, more intense interval sessions may improve performance.

VO2max - Your Aerobic Potential - Endurance training and VO2 max seem to be inextricably linked.

Heart Rate Training for Endurance Events - Heart rate training, despite being erratic, is still popular with cyclists. Cardiac drift is a phenomenon in which heart rate increases over the period of exercise, even if intensity does not.

Altitude Training - Performance can be improved through altitude training.

The Sport-Specific Approach to Strength Training Programs - Strength training is suitable for all the cycling disciplines, even ultra distance road cyclists. But a strength training program must match the demands of the event it's designed for.

Power Training for Athletes - It may be obvious that track and speedway cyclists must be powerful to be successful in their events, however, even distance cyclists require explosive power for mass starts, hill climbing and sprint finishes. So what are the best methods for improving explosive power?

Plyometric Training for Sport-Specific Power - Plyometrics is one very effective form of power training.

Muscular Endurance Training - While explosive power is key in the sprint events, muscular endurance is equally as important in distance events.

Flexibility Exercises - Flexibility training is part and parcel of most athletes' conditioning program. Increased flexibility may reduce the risk of certain long-term injuries.

Self Myofascial Release Exercises - Many Exercise Scientists believe that enhancing recovery between training sessions is the key to winning. Myofascial release exercises are said to relieve and release trigger points in the muscle sheath that may compound leading to injury and sub-optimal performance.

The Wingate Test - One of the most reliable tests for anaerobic power and capacity.

More information can be obtained at reference link below:

http://www.sport-fitness-advisor.com/cycling-training.html

Fig 20: Riders training at Kissena

Fit Test
It has been about one month now since I started the gym,
transitioning into weight lifing and detraining the cycling
muscles. On 9/26/2009 I did a base line fit test at home. Today I
did the same fit test in the gym - all the scores have improved,
except the recovery pulse after a 3 minute step test - this is
understandable since I am not doing interval training at the
moment.

Body weight - 175 lbs.

Test - Pull Ups with palms facing in
Quantity = 15
Score - average
Measures upper body strength and endurance.

Test - Vertical Leap
Quantity = 22 inches
Score - above average
Measures lower body power levels.

Test - Push Ups
Quantity = 62
Score - Excellent
Measures muscular strength and endurance.

Test - Sit & Reach Toes
Quantity = +3 1/2 inches past toes
Score - Good
Measures flexibility of the lower back and hamstring.

Test - Wall Sit isometric
Quantity = 2 minutes 30 seconds
Score - Excellent
Measures quadriceps strength and endurance.

Test - In & Out crunches
Quantity = 100
Score - Excellent
Measures abdominal strength and endurance

Test - Standing Long Jump
Quantity = 7'-5"
Score - Average
Measures explosive power of the legs

Test - 3 minute Step Test - HR 166
Quantity = HR after 1 min 156 bpm
Score - Very Poor

How to develop a training program
The process of creating a training program to help develop an
individual's level of fitness comprises of 6 stages:

- Stage 1 - gather details about the individual
- Stage 2 - identify the fitness components to develop
- Stage 3 - identify appropriate tests to monitor fitness status
- Stage 4 - conduct a gap analysis
- Stage 5 - compile the program
- Stage 6 - monitor progress and adjust program

Stage 1

The first stage is to gather details about the individual:

- Age
- Reasons for wanting to get fit
- Current or recent injuries
- Health problems
- The sports they play and how often
- Their dislikes and likes with regards to training
- What sports facilities they have access to - gym, sports center.

Prior to starting any training, it is recommended you have a medical examination to ensure it is safe for you to do so.

Stage 2

The second stage is to determine what components of fitness they need to improve. This will depend upon what the individual wants to get fit for - to improve general fitness, get fit enough to play in the Saturday hockey league, run a local 5 km fun run or compete in next year's London Marathon. Exercise scientists have identified nine elements that comprise the definition of fitness. The following lists each of the nine elements and an example of how they are used:

- Strength - the extent to which muscles can exert force by contracting against resistance (holding or restraining an object or person)

- Power - the ability to exert maximum muscular contraction instantly in an explosive burst of movements (Jumping or sprint starting)

- Agility - the ability to perform a series of explosive power movements in rapid succession in opposing directions (ZigZag running or cutting movements)

- Balance - the ability to control the body's position, either stationary (e.g. a handstand) or while moving (e.g. a gymnastics stunt)

- Flexibility - the ability to achieve an extended range of motion without being impeded by excess tissue, i.e. fat or muscle (Executing a leg split)

- Local Muscle Endurance - a single muscle's ability to perform sustained work (Rowing or cycling)

- Cardiovascular Endurance - the heart's ability to deliver blood to working muscles and their ability to use it (Running long distances)

- Strength Endurance - a muscle's ability to perform a maximum contracture time after time (Continuous explosive rebounding through an entire basketball game)

- Coordination - the ability to integrate the above listed components so that effective movements are achieved

Of all the nine elements of fitness cardiac respiratory qualities are the most important to develop as they enhance all the other components of the conditioning equation. You will need to consider which of these elements are applicable to the individuals training program based on what it is they want to get fit for.

Stage 3
The next stage is to identify appropriate tests that can be used to initially determine the individual's level of fitness and then to monitor progress during the training.

Stage 4
We now know the individual's background, objectives and current level of fitness. We now need to conduct a gap analysis of the current fitness levels and target fitness levels. The results of this process will assist in the design of the training program so that each component of fitness is improved to the desired level.

Stage 5
The next stage is to prepare a training program using the results of the gap analysis and FITT principles.

F - frequency - how often should the individual exercise?
I - intensity - how hard should the individual exercise?
T - time - how long should each session last?
T - training activity - what exercise or training activity will help achieve the individual's fitness goals?

For frequency, intensity and time you should start at an easy level and increase gradually e.g. 10% increments. Aerobic training should last for 20 to 40 minutes. Strength work should last 15 to 30 minutes and comprise of 3 sessions a week with 48 hours recovery between sessions.

Plan the program in four week cycles where the workload in the first three weeks increase each week (easy, medium, hard) and the fourth week comprises of active recovery and tests to monitor training progress. The aim of the four week cycles is to:

- Build you up to a level of fitness (3 weeks)
- Test, recovery and adjustment of the training program (1 week)
- Build you up to higher level of fitness (3 weeks)

- Test, recovery and adjustment of the training program (1 week)
- Build you up to an even higher level of fitness (3 weeks) and so on

The tests used to assess the individual's initial level of fitness should be planned into week 4 of the program in order to monitor progress and effectiveness of the program. The test results can be used to adjust the program accordingly.

The program needs to last 12 to 16 weeks in order to see any real benefits and the planning (initial & subsequent adjustments) should be conducted with the individual so that they feel they own the program. This will ensure the program is enjoyable and convenient to do.

Stage 6
The program has now been agreed and the individual can undertake the program and evaluate the program:
- How the training has gone
- The test results
- Progress towards target fitness levels
- Adjustments to the training program

More information can be obtained at reference link below
http://www.brianmac.co.uk/plant.htm

Fig 21: The intensity of a race at Kissena

Graded exercise test to determine Lactate Threshold:
One of the measures to be gleaned from the graded exercise test is your lactate threshold heart rate and power on the spin bike. Extracted from Joel Friel's - The Cyclist Training Bible.

You start at a 100 watts (plus or minus 10 watts) and increase output by 20 watts every minute until it becomes too difficult to maintain the effort.

-Minute 1 - 102 watts - 147 bpm - 8 exertion
-Minute 2 - 122 watts - 156 bpm - 9 exertion
-Minute 3 - 169 watts - 162 bpm - 11 exertion
-Minute 4 - 178 watts - 165 bpm - 13 exertion
-Minute 5 - 210 watts - 170 bpm - 14 exertion
-Minute 6 - 225 watts - 175 bpm - 15 exertion
-Minute 7 - 245 watts - 180 bpm - 17 exertion - VT
-Minute 8 - 290 watts - 185 bpm - 19 exertion
-Minute 9 - 320 watts - 190 bpm - 20 exertion

Ventilation Threshold (VT) is when your breathing becomes labored.

Perceived Exertion Guide:
-1
-2
-3
-4
-5
-6
-7 = very very light
-8
-9 = very light
-10
-11 = fairly light
-12
-13 = somewhat hard
-14
-15 = hard
-16
-17 = very hard
-18
-19 = very very hard
-20

Sprint Power Test

This test is done on a spin bike with a power and heart rate meter. You first warm up, then do a couple of powerful starts of 8 to 12 seconds to determine the best resistance to do the test in. You will then recover and sprint all out for 322 meters which should take you about 25 to 40 seconds. At the end of the test record the maximum watts and average watts. Warm down by spinning at low resistance.

If you score a 4 or 5, the quick application of force and lactate tolerance are among your strength areas. Average power output will vary throughout the year than will maximum power. While testing in the winter, for example, you may find average power relatively lower than in the summer when race fitness is high. That is because you quickly lose the ability to tolerate lactate in the winter when the body is no longer experiencing it. Extracted from Joel Friel's - The Cyclist Training Bible.

Sprint Power Test data from data below, conducted on Cyclops spin bike during the winter:

- Speed max = 32.54 mph
  Speed avg = 22.27 mph

- Cadence max = 131 rpm
  Cadence avg = 90 rpm

- Heart max = 186 bpm
  Heart avg = 174 bpm

- Torque max = 23.73 nm
  Torque avg = 16.46 nm

- Power max = 896 watts
  Power avg = 579 watts

- Power watts/kg max = 11.28 watts
  Power watts/kg avg = 7.29 watts

Ranking scores:
- Excellent = 5
- Good = 4
- **Average = 3**
- Fair = 2
- Poor = 1

Based on the above data this is how I currently rank:
- Ranking = Average for Senior Men
  Score = 3
- Maximum watts range = 800 to 949 (mine 896)
- Average watts range = 560 to 664 (mine 579)

Fig 22: A very fast junior woman rider at Kissena

Functional Threshold Power - FTP Test:
Cycling and training has certainly become more sophisticated / complicated over the years. Whatever happened to riding a bike based solely on perceived effort? Having a pulse watch back in the 80s was considered cutting edge technology. Now we have power meters and GPS devices, interpreting data is like being in a Physics class once again.

Today (12/8/2012) I will be doing a Functional Threshold Power (FTP) test on a spin bike. FTP is basically your Anaerobic Threshold level or Lactate Threshold.

A Functional Threshold Power test as described in the book "Training and Racing with a Power Meter" by Hunter Allen and Andrew Coggan. Below is a summary of what has to be done.

- 20 minute warm up at about 65% max heart rate.
- 3 x 1 minute fast pedals at 100 rpm with 1 minute rest between efforts.
- 5 minute easy at 65% max heart rate.
- 5 minutes all out.

- 10 minutes easy at 65% max heart rate.
- **20 minutes time trial, gradually build up to speed and hold it pushing very hard last 3 minutes.**
- 10 minutes easy at 65% max heart rate.
- 10 minutes cool down at easy pace.

The average power in the 20 minute segment will be my Functional Threshold Power, this would be the base line from where my training levels will be determined and improvements monitored. Technically the test should be done for 60 minutes to get a more accurate number. Since this test has to be repeated over time it was then broken down to 20 minutes to prevent riders from dreading the test, 5% is subtracted from the number to compensate for the shorter duration.

FTP test done 12/8/2012

Zones	Description	Power Range	Heart Range
1	Active Recovery	1-118 watts	less than 117
2	Endurance	120-161 watts	119 – 144
3	Tempo	163-193 watts	145 – 163
4	Lactate Threshold	195 – 225 watts	164 – 182
5	Vo2 Max	229 – 258 watts	184
6	Anaerobic Capacity	260 – 322 watts	n/a
7	NeuroMuscular	n/a	n/a

Note:
- Weight 165 lbs
- Body fat 13%

Based on 20 minute FTP test with an average power of 226 watts minus 5% = 215 Watts. Power and heart rate ranges above are based on 215 watts and 173 bpm. I did this test after 75 days of the 90 day P90X classic functional training program with hardly any riding on the bicycle. The results are relatively close to Joel Friel's graded exercise test to determine lactate threshold.

Fig 23: The officials keeping an eye on the riders at Kissena

The whole point of training is to be able to put out a lot of power at a low body weight and heart rate, this will result in going faster and longer on a bicycle. So even though my 30 second sprint power test is impressive my FTP threshold is low. In order to take advantage of my high max power I need to do high cadence work such as flying 100 meters and 200 meters in small gears (82 to 84 inches) on the track and high cadence work on the road in small gears accelerating downhill. Always remember that high power does not mean pushing big gears, it is about being efficient at a lean body mass and riding your optimal cadence. At a body weight of 165 lbs (75 Kilograms), my power output is about **2.9 Watts per Kilogram** (215 Watts divided by 75 Kilograms). A 225 lbs rider (102 Kilograms) can have a higher FTP of 270 Watts but that doesn't mean he is going to beat you because his Watts per Kilogram of body weight is only **2.6 Watts per Kilogram** (270 Watts divided by 102 Kilograms). He will probably beat you in a short sprint, but not on a long distance ride, or hilly ride.

Power:

Power is the rate at which energy is used (energy over time) and is measured in Watts. A watt is a watt, whether on a bike or powering your home.

Average Power:
Your average power output over the whole ride, just like your average speed readout.

KiloJoules:
The basic unit of work, one kJ becomes roughly equal to a kilocalorie (or what nutritionists just call a calorie). The actual rate is 4.18kJs = 1 calorie, but people range from 20-25 percent efficiency. So for every, say, 100 calories burned in exercise, only 20 to 25 propel you forward and are measured at the power meter.

Functional Threshold Power (FTP):
This is a vital measurement of how much power you can sustainably produce over a one-hour period and is a fundamental metric of fitness. It's often expressed in watts produced per kilogram of body weight.

Normalized Power:
Since power meters record zero power during coasting, that's factored into your average power output over the duration of a ride. Normalized power strips out the coasting sections, so you get an accurate average power number for only the portion of your ride you were pedaling. It will always be higher than average power. Average power is still important, however; compared with normalized power and ride duration, you can get a sense for how intense the ride was.

Fig 24: Riders getting ready for a Team Sprint at Kissena

Training Stress Score:

TrainingPeaks developed this metric, called Training Stress Score (TSS), which measures the relative intensity of a ride, by measuring how much of your threshold power you produced and for how long. It's relative to the rider by fitness, not size, so two equal-size riders could get a different score for the same ride if their fitness varies. An all-out one-hour effort gets a TSS of 100. Two hours, hard, is 150 and a century is about 225. A typical Tour stage can be anywhere from 250 to 400. TSS is valuable for determining when you've gone extremely deep and need to recover, and TrainingPeaks feels that for training, it's a more exact metric than kiloJoules of workload for a particular rider.

Watts/Kg:
Raw watts aren't the most reliable metric of performance, because riders put out varying levels. A better measure, especially on climbs, is watts produced per kilogram of body weight (that normalizes the size difference).

Heart Rate:
Just because power is more exact a measurement of training doesn't mean you give up on heart rate (HR). It still matters because this is your body's response to the work. And it's an important barometer of how you feel. Let's say you go ride and on a climb you feel awful; your heart rate spikes but your power just isn't there. You might be overtrained, or getting sick. An unusually high HR signals that something's not right; you won't get much out of training today so you should head home and let your body rest.

Cadence:
So there are two ways to increase your power: You can boost the actual force on the pedal, or you can increase the number of times the pedal goes around in a minute. That is cadence. You'll notice if you ride with a power meter that when you downshift and pedal a higher cadence, it might feel a little easier at first, but your power actually increases. Even though you're not putting the same amount of force into each pedal stroke, the increase in cadence means there are more pedal strokes per minute. So, more total power.

Chapter 4 – Energy Systems

I will make a little comparison between an airplane power plant and the human body for later reference when I speak about altitude and air density in Chapter 10. This was learnt in ground school in preparation for the Private Pilot test. The airplane power plant and the human body are heat machines, just like any heat engine the human body needs fuel. Humans consume fuel in the form of carbohydrates, proteins and fats found in food, oxidation then converts this fuel to the heat and energy we need to live.

Oxidation is a burning process and requires Oxygen. Oxygen is extracted from the air by the lungs and is distributed through the body by the circulation system. Air is a mixture of several gases – 21% Oxygen, 78% Nitrogen and 1% other gases. The percentage of Oxygen remains fairly constant up to the lower levels of the stratosphere. At sea level a healthy person can extract enough oxygen from the air to maintain normal activities. However, at 8,000 or 9,000 feet above sea level problems caused by a shortage of oxygen begin because the air is less dense therefore the body assimilates less oxygen even though the ratio of oxygen to nitrogen is still the same as at sea level. Total pressure or more importantly the partial pressure of Oxygen has been reduced. As blood circulates it picks up Oxygen from the lungs and transports the Oxygen to the tissues and carries Carbon Dioxide back to the lungs where it is exhaled. The amount of Oxygen the blood can pick up and haul to the tissues depends on a large measure on the pressure the Oxygen exerts on the blood as it passes through the lungs. When air is inhaled at high altitudes there isn't enough Oxygen pressure to force it through the membranes of the lungs into the blood stream. This condition when the body lacks sufficient Oxygen is called Hypoxia:

- **Ischemic Hypoxia** – reduction of blood flow through the tissue.

- **Histotoxic Hypoxia** – interference in ability of tissues to utilize oxygen and may be caused by alcohol or drugs.
- **Hypemic Hypoxia** – reduction in oxygen carrying capacity of the blood and may be caused by smoking.
- **Hypoxic Hypoxia** – reduction of oxygen entering the blood an caused by exposure to altitude.

At 10,000 feet the blood can still pick up 90% of its capacity of Oxygen, at that altitude a person can become slightly impaired after some time and be less able to concentrate. At 14,000 feet a healthy person will be severely impaired and disregard hazardous situations. At 18,000 and feet and above, exposure to environmental air will cause total collapse of the human physiological functions and loss of useful consciousness. That is why airplanes are pressurized at altitude to maintain acceptable pressure for the body to use Oxygen, or supplemental Oxygen has to be used continuously. That is why training at altitude will make your body increase the production of red blood cells to make use of the limited Oxygen supplied to your body due to a decrease in pressure. More on pressure and air density in Chapter 10, time to talk about energy systems in the human body.

The Energy Systems:
In order to determine how energy is produced in our muscles we have to consider some important factors:

"Is air, in the form of oxygen, required?"
If it is, we say the energy system is aerobic.
If not, it is anaerobic.

"Is lactic acid produced?"
If it is, we say the system is lactic.
If not, and no air is required, it is alactic.

So, there are three energy systems operating in the body. One of these is aerobic, with oxygen and two are anaerobic, without oxygen:

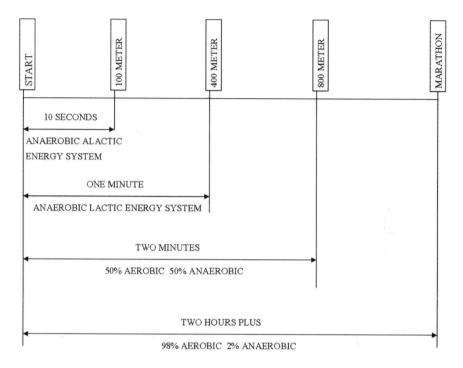

Fig 25: Correlation of energy systems with time duration.

1. Aerobic System
The muscle energy system which requires oxygen.

2. Anaerobic Alactic System
The stored, start up system which does not require oxygen and does not produce lactic acid.

3. Anaerobic Lactic System
The system which does not require oxygen but produces lactic acid.

The athlete's body is capable of using one or any combination of the three energy systems. Different events demand different types and amounts of muscle activity. Consequently, different

57

energy systems predominate in the various events. Improving performance is often the result of carefully designed training programs that aim to increase the capability of specific energy systems and muscles.

Fig 26: Riders getting ready for a Team Sprint at Kissena

The Aerobic-Anaerobic Split
The aerobic-anaerobic split refers to how much the aerobic and anaerobic energy systems are involved in a particular activity. Marathon runners, for example, produce most of their energy aerobically, while sprinters, jumpers and throwers depend more on anaerobic sources. The aerobic- anaerobic split is determined by identifying how long and how hard our athletes work without rest.

There are two important work times that mark a shift in emphasis from one of the three energy systems to another:

10 seconds--After 10 seconds of intense muscular activity the energy system providing the majority of the energy shifts from

the anaerobic alactic to the anaerobic lactic system.

1 minute---After about 1 minute of intense activity the shift is away from the anaerobic lactic system to the aerobic system as is the case in the Kilometer time trial on the track.

1. The Aerobic Endurance Energy System
The aerobic system requires oxygen. This system is used in lower intensity exercise and is the basic system which provides the energy for most human activity from birth to death. As such it is also important in recovery from exercise of all intensities. It is very efficient and does not produce fatigue producing waste products. The heart and lungs are important in aerobic activity as oxygen and fuel are carried to the muscles in the blood.

The aerobic system resists fatigue. It takes longer to overload than either of the anaerobic systems. Training the aerobic energy system must be a minimum of 20 minutes duration. The work load for aerobic training can be either continuous or broken up into intervals of harder and easier efforts. Correct aerobic training will improve aerobic energy production in the muscle and also improve the support of the heart and lungs, the oxygen transport system.

2. Anaerobic Alactic Energy
The 'First 10 Seconds' Energy
The anaerobic alactic system is the one referred to as the stored or start up energy system. This system provides the majority of energy when our athletes do bursts of high speed or high resistance movements lasting up to 10 seconds. The stores of energy in the muscle which are used up in the intense burst of activity return to normal levels within 2 - 3 minutes of rest. As is the case when working on standing starts and all out short sprints.

The anaerobic alactic energy system is developed by alternating periods of work and rest. The work time should be very intense, but not exceed 10 seconds, as this is the limit of the energy

59

system. The rest periods should be 1½ to 3 minutes, depending on the duration of intense activity, to allow the muscle energy stores to build up again. If an athlete shows the effects of fatigue, allow more rest time or decrease the work time.

3. Anaerobic Lactic Energy
The '10 Seconds to One Minute' Energy System

This energy system is capable of high levels of intensity, but this intensity prevents the removal of waste products because not enough oxygen is available. The system operates without oxygen. As a result lactic acid accumulates within muscle cells and blood. This is a major cause of fatigue, which eventually slows the athlete. The more intense the exercise rate, the faster the rate of lactic acid accumulation to high fatigue causing levels. For example, the 400 meter runner will accumulate high levels of lactic acid after 35-40 seconds. The 800 meter runner runs more slowly and accumulates lactic acid at a slower rate, reaching high levels after about 70-85 seconds. Training for track cycling follows the same principles as training for some track and field events.

Getting rid of lactic acid after activity is a much slower process than the replacement of energy stores in the anaerobic alactic system. It may take more than one hour for lactic acid levels to return to their pre-exercise level. Light activity such as walking or jogging following intense efforts speeds up the removal of lactic acid. The first ten minutes of active recovery produces the greatest reduction in lactic acid levels.

The anaerobic lactic energy system is developed by intense work loads of 10 seconds to two minutes duration. Rest periods will depend on the duration of the work and should be three to ten minutes to allow removal of most of the lactic acid produced.

Why do we train Energy Systems:

The **Basal Metabolic Rate** (BMR) is the minimum amount of energy we require to stay alive, and is measured by monitoring oxygen and CO2 excretion.

ATP - Adenosine Triphosphate

ATP = ADP + P + Energy (ADP - Adenosine Diphospate)

Muscles store enough ATP for a 2 second contraction - this would supply sufficient energy for muscle contractions of short duration such as required for weight lifting, power lifting and shot putting.

Energy is released when a phosphate is broken off the ATP returning it to ADP. The cycle is continuous, with ADP being converted back to ATP.

ATP breaks down to release energy when a nerve impulse stimulates a muscle fiber. The energy used from the breakdown of food joins a phosphate ion to ADP via a high energy bond.

There are three energy systems in the body that produce ATP. These are:

The aerobic system - releases energy slowly by using oxygen to breaking down glucose. It provides lots of long term energy suitable for every day activities and endurance events. It can also break down fat to make ATP. As we get fitter, the amount of oxygen used by muscles increases. Energy is produced by the mitochondria. Byproducts are water, which we sweat or urine, and CO2, which we exhale.

The anaerobic systems, which produce energy without oxygen. These are:

The Phosphate System - the creatine phosphate molecule can be broken down quickly and is used to turn ADP back into ATP. The phosphate system is suitable for single or continuous short bursts of energy of around 10 seconds (as soon as ATP is broken down to ADP it is restored to ATP). This system would be used for events such as the long jump and javelin. The amount of creatine phosphate in muscles is limited, which is why athletes often use creatine phosphate supplements. This system is also called the ATP/PC system, the Alactate Anaerobic System and the ATP + CP system.

The Lactic Acid System - Provides energy for a longer duration than the Phosphate System, between 10 - 90 seconds, such as what would be required for a 100m swim, or a 400-800m run. Energy is derived from the fast break down of glucose from glycogen and blood sugar. Glycogen is stored in the liver and the muscles. When glycogen is broken down, it produces ATP and pyruvic acid. This process is called anaerobic glycolysis because the glycogen isn't fully broken down, but leaves a byproduct called Lactic Acid. When lactic acid accumulates in the muscles it results in muscle fatigue and weakness.

Factors Contributing to Muscle Fatigue
- Excessive activity - accumulation of lactic acid and CO_2.
- Malnutrition - insufficient glucose to muscles.
- Cardiovascular anomalies - poor circulation affecting delivery of glucose and oxygen, and the removal of waste products.
- Respiratory anomalies - insufficient oxygen

System	What is broken down	How long
Aerobic	Glycogen, fat	Long term
Phosphate	Creatine Phosphate	Up to 10 seconds
Lactic Acid	Glycogen	Approx 1.5 minutes

Before you get into a high intensity training such as intervals and speed work as noted in the next chapter, you will have to lay an aerobic base on which to build on. This would entail riding at a steady pace for about 2 or more hours in your Zone 2 intensity range, where it is not too hard nor too easy. You can still carry on a conversation, but at the same time you body is adapting to the aerobic training by using more oxygen and burning more fat as fuel. These rides will build more capillaries, the tiny blood vessels that deliver oxygen rich blood to your muscles. Your mitochondria – the parts of your cells that produce energy – also multiply and enlarge, and your body creates more enzymes that help turn stored fuel such as fat into energy. The result is you can ride faster and longer. So keep it steady during these rides. You can also develop strength during the base period on the bike by doing some one hour hill climbs at a lower cadence in the saddle which will build hip and knee strength and improve power.

Fig 27: Riders getting ready for a training effort at Kissena

Weight training can also help to develop strength and power off the bike. The base building period usually last about three months. Without the base miles, you will not be able to sustain your training or maximize the higher intensity training to come later. If you go right into speed work, you will definitely get fast on the bike, but you won't have the endurance to sustain your fitness levels. Also you will not be able to repeat hard efforts without a solid endurance base. Please note the last 200 meters of a kilo time trial is purely aerobic, so the endurance training comes into play here.

The best investment you make for this type of training during the winter is a spin bike with power meter. It not only allows you to train indoors and monitor your progress, but it also allows you to really apply maximal force and put in huge efforts without worrying about breaking something on your regular bicycle which is mounted to a trainer or on rollers. A spin bike is especially useful during standing starts and sprint efforts during interval training. The utility from a spin bike is much more than you will get from an expensive disk wheel, which only gives you a marginal advantage considering the cost of the wheel. You can also make your training more effective by doing a Metabolic test to see how energy is used in your body.

What is Resting Metabolic Rate (RMR)
Metabolism, quite simply, is the conversion of food to energy. Metabolic rate is a measure of how much food, or fat, is converted to energy in a day. Resting metabolic rate (RMR) is the measurement of how much food, or energy, is required to maintain basic body functions such as heartbeat, breathing, and maintenance of body heat while you are in a state of rest. That energy is expressed in calories per day. So an RMR measurement shows how many calories you burn at rest, doing nothing more than sitting in a chair.

How Metabolic Testing Works
Indirect calorimetry (a measurement of metabolic rate) relies on the fact that burning 1 calorie (Kilocalorie) requires 208.06 milliliters of oxygen. Because of this very direct relationship between caloric burn and oxygen consumed, measurements of oxygen uptake (VO2) and caloric burn rate are virtually interchangeable. Oxygen uptake requires a precise measurement of the volume of expired air and of the concentrations of oxygen in the inspired and expired air. The process requires that all of the air a person breathes out be collected and analyzed while they rest quietly.

Fig 28: Rider warming up on a turbo trainer at Kissena

Chapter 5 – Training Protocols

Delayed Onset Muscle Soreness – DOMS
Starting a workout program can be challenging. Making the time to exercise, creating a balanced routine, and setting goals are hard enough, but add to that the muscle soreness that comes with adapting to that regimen, and it may be difficult to stay on track. Chances are, you won't be leaping out of bed to get to the gym when it hurts to hold your arm up to brush your teeth.
After participating in some kind of strenuous physical activity, particularly something new to your body, it is common to experience muscle soreness, say experts.

Exercise physiologists refer to the gradually increasing discomfort that occurs between 24 and 48 hours after activity as delayed onset muscle soreness (DOMS), and it is perfectly normal.

"Delayed onset muscle soreness (DOMS) is a common result of physical activity that stresses the muscle tissue beyond what it is accustomed to," says David O. Draper, professor and director of the graduate program in sports medicine/athletic training at Brigham Young University in Provo, Utah.

To be more specific, says Draper, who's also a member of the heat-responsive pain council, delayed onset muscle soreness occurs when the muscle is performing an eccentric or a lengthening contraction. Examples of this would be running downhill or the lengthening portion of a bicep curl.
"Small microscopic tears occur in the muscle," he says.
The mild muscle strain injury creates microscopic damage to the muscle fibers. Scientists believe this damage, coupled with the inflammation that accompanies these tears, causes the pain.
"The aches and pains should be minor," says Carol Torgan, an exercise physiologist and fellow of the American College of Sports Medicine, "and are simply indications that muscles are adapting to your fitness regimen."

Fig 29: Rider cooling down on a turbo trainer at Kissena

Even Bodybuilders Get Them
No one is immune to muscle soreness. Exercise neophytes and bodybuilders alike experience delayed onset muscle soreness. "Anyone can get cramps or DOMS, from weekend warriors to elite athletes," says Torgan. "The muscle discomfort is simply a symptom of using your muscles and placing stresses on them that are leading to adaptations to make them stronger and better able to perform the task the next time."

Ease Those Aching Muscles
So what can you do to alleviate the pain?
"Exercise physiologists and athletic trainers have not yet
discovered a panacea for DOMS," says Draper, "however,
several remedies such as ice, rest, anti-inflammatory medication,
massage, heat, and stretch have been reported as helpful in the
process of recovery."

Stretching and flexibility are underrated, says Sharp.
"People don't stretch enough," he says. "Stretching helps break
the cycle," which goes from soreness to muscle spasm to
contraction and tightness.

Take it easy for a few days while your body adapts, says Torgan.
Or try some light exercise such as walking or swimming, she
suggests. Keeping the muscle in motion can also provide some
relief.

"Probably the most important thing is to have a cool-down phase
after your workout," says Draper. Right before finishing, include
10 or so minutes of "easy aerobic work such as jogging or
walking followed by stretching."

"When muscle temperature is increased, blood flow increases,
bringing fresh oxygen and healing nutrients to the injured site,"
he says. "This increased blood flow also helps to wash away the
chemical irritants responsible for pain."

While sore, don't expect to set personal records. Most likely,
during a bout of DOMS, your exercise potential will be out of
reach, says Draper. Delayed onset muscle soreness usually
affects only the body parts that were worked, so perhaps you can
work other muscle groups while letting the fatigued ones
recover.

In a nutshell, don't beat yourself up. Just take it easy.

"Since there's a loss in muscle strength, athletic performance won't be at peak levels for a few days," says Torgan, "so it's best to plan a few days of easy exercise to prevent further muscle damage and reduce the likelihood of injury."

It's also a process of muscle conditioning. Torgan says delayed onset muscle soreness also has a "repeated bouts" effect.
"If someone does an activity, they will be inoculated for a few weeks to a few months -- the next time they do the activity, there will be less muscle tissue damage, less soreness, and a faster strength recovery."

This is why athletes often cross-train and vary their routines to continue to challenge and develop their muscle strength.
It is important to distinguish the difference between moderate muscle soreness induced by exercise and muscle overuse or injury.

"If soreness prevents you from performing daily activities associated with living and work, then that is too much soreness," Draper says. "It can psychologically deter someone from continuing a workout program."

Both Draper and Torgan stress that soreness is not necessary to see improvements."There are all kinds of different little roads that your muscles can take to get stronger," says Torgan. Regardless of whether you're sore, there are still improvements occurring in your muscles during exercise.

However, moderate muscle pain might go a long way to keeping someone on the path to fitness."Soreness can serve as encouragement in a workout program because people like immediate results. Muscle doesn't visibly [grow] overnight; nor does your time in the mile drop from eight to six minutes," says Draper. "So something like soreness can give people encouragement that they are in fact working the muscle."

More information can be found at reference link below:

Fig 30: Riders getting ready for the annual Kissena 150 lap ride

Muscle fibers:
Slow- twitch fibers are identified by a slow contraction time and a high resistance to fatigue.

Fast-twitch fibers are identified by a quick contraction time and a low resistance to fatigue.

As mentioned before the key component which makes our muscles contract is ATP – Adenosine Triphosphate. There are three energy systems in the body that produce ATP – the aerobic system, the anaerobic or phosphate system and the lactic acid system.

Summary of training your energy systems:
Aerobic system: Sustained aerobic activity (20-40 minutes). A base of aerobic training has to be in place before moving on to Phosphate and Anaerobic training.

Phosphate system: Short 10 second sprints and low volume high weight sets (4-7 reps). Complete rest of 5 to 25 minutes is required in between sets to allow for full recovery and to prevent the build up of too much lactic acid. This allows you to perform at maximal intensities. This type of training is for Match Sprinting events.

Lactic Acid Anaerobic system: Extended sprints and mid range resistance (8-12 reps). This type of training can be applied to the Kilo or 500 meter time trial events.

Training varies according to the type and number of events being raced. Sprint track cyclists generally focus on short high quality repetitions with long recovery, as well as strength training to build lean body mass. For longer sprint events, athletes also include some longer sessions and endurance rides. Longer track events such as the Points Race, Madison, and Keirin are generally suited to endurance trained road cyclists, who compete on the track in the off season. With a good endurance base and short periods of sprint training, road cyclists can excel in track endurance events.

A good kilo rider may only be average at the sprint and a sprinter may find the kilo to be too long. Sprinters are primarily concerned with developing the Phosphate System. To do this they will do a lot of short but very intense efforts typically around 10 seconds in duration. This will increase muscular strength of the fast twitch muscles and increase the amount of ATP available.

You have to train the aerobic system with high aerobic mileage for track events. To do this you have to do a lot of winter miles with your heart rate 60 to 70% of your maximum. Usually road rides no longer than two hours or forty miles in one session. These are called base miles, then as you get within a few months of racing, you start doing shorter but harder efforts. You need to know your anaerobic threshold to do these effectively, start by doing 10 to 20 minutes 5 beats per minute below your anaerobic threshold. Increase the time or number of sets for a while. Then do some efforts closer to anaerobic threshold, then right at anaerobic threshold, then a little above. Many riders become sprinters so they can avoid efforts like this. You will also need to develop your lactic acid system to survive when the pace picks up during an endurance event. Hard efforts that take between 1 to 3 minutes is one good way of developing the lactic acid system, doing lots of racing will also work.

Interval Training
This is a type of discontinuous physical training that involves a series of low- to high-intensity exercise workouts interspersed with rest or relief periods. The high-intensity periods are typically at or close to anaerobic threshold, while the recovery periods involve activity of lower intensity.

Interval training can be described as short periods of work followed by rest. The main aim is to improve speed and cardiovascular fitness.

Interval training can refer to organization of any cardiovascular workout (e.g., cycling, running, rowing, etc), and is prominent in training routines for many sports. It is a technique particularly employed by runners, but athletes from several backgrounds have been known to use this type of training.

Interval training is a favorite of coaches because of its effectiveness in cardiovascular build-up and also its ability to make more well-rounded runners and riders. However, it is also applicable to exercisers as it helps improve exercisers' aerobic capacity to exercise longer at varying intensities (Mayo Clinic, 2009).

Interval training can be an effective means of enhancing an athlete's lactate threshold. Lactate threshold has been shown to be a significant factor determining performance for long distance running events.

This method of training may be more effective at inducing fat loss than simply training at a moderate intensity level for the same duration. This is due to the metabolism boosting effects of high intensity intervals. P90X is a great program for this as will be discussed later. This is definitely a plug for P90X because it works.

A typical routine for Endurance training on the spin bike is as follows:
- 10 minute warm up
- 10 minute x 90 rpms in your endurance heart range
- 10 minute x 70 rpms in your endurance heart range
- 10 minute x 90 rpms in your endurance heart range
- 10 minute x 70 rpms in your endurance heart range
- 10 minute x 90 rpms in your endurance heart range
- 10 minute x 70 rpms in your endurance heart range
- 10 minute warm down

A typical routine for Kilo Training is as follows:
- 20 minute warm up.
- Standing 10 second sprints with 10 to 12 minute full recovery
- Rolling 10 second sprints with10 to 12 minute full recovery
- 2 to 4 intervals at 4 to 5 minutes in length targeting your VO2 max with 4 to 5 minute rest.
- 20 minutes at Lactate Threshold
- 10 minute warm down

This is probably the optimal order, working on sprints when you are freshest. But as you get closer to your event you can start with the longer stuff and finish with the sprints so that you are mimicking what goes on in a race.

Base information for sprinters:
An important test of strength is the two legged triple jump

73

measured together to give total distance. This is done 3 to 4 times a year to track improvements in strength.

Leg speed or revolutions per minute is also another test for sprinters. A sprinter should be able to pedal at high rpm on the track and be capable of higher rpm on a free running spin bike with no load.

A typical routine for Sprint Strength Training is as follows:
- 20 minute warm up
- Roll off the banking and start at the finish line
- 100 meters flying starts, 2 sets of 5 reps maximal
- 5 minute recovery between reps
- 10 minutes recovery between sets
  Gear range varies from 82" to 88"
  (82,84,84,84,84,84,86,86,88,88)
- Rpm 140 to 160
- Time to complete each rep 5 to 6 seconds
- 10 minute warm down in small gear

A typical routine for Sprint Endurance Training is as follows:
- 20 minute warm up
- Roll off the banking
- 300 meters flying start – 6 reps sub maximal
- 5 to 10 minutes recovery between reps
- Gears 82, 82, 84,84,86,86
- Rpm 135 to 160
- Time to complete each rep 16 to 20 seconds.
- 10 minute warm down in small gear

A typical routine for Speed Strength Endurance Training is as follows:
- 20 minute warm up
- Roll off the banking
- 500 meter flying start – 4 to 6 reps sub maximal

- 10 minutes recovery between reps
- Gears 84 to 92
- Rpm 130 – 145
- Time to complete each rep 29 to 37 seconds
- 10 minute warm down in small gear

A typical routine for Speed Endurance Training on the spin bike is as follows:
- 10 minute warm up
- 1 minute x 110 rpms at 90% effort (moderate resistance)
- 2 minutes rest easy spin
- Repeat 10 times
- 5 minutes rest easy spin
- 1 minute x 110 rpms at 90% effort (moderate resistance)
- 2 minutes rest easy spin
- Repeat 10 times
- 5 minute rest easy spin
- 1 minute x 110 rpms at 90% effort (moderate resistance)
- 2 minutes rest easy spin
- 10 minute warm down

Another routine for Speed Endurance Training on the spin bike is as follows:
- 10 minute warm up
- 30 seconds x 120 rpms at 90% effort (moderate resistance)
- 1 minute rest easy spin
- Repeat 10 times
- Rest 5 minutes easy spin
- 30 seconds x 120 rpms at 90% effort (moderate resistance)
- 1 minute rest easy spin
- Repeat 10 times
- Rest 5 minutes easy spin
- 30 seconds x 120 rpms at 90% effort (moderate resistance)

- 1 minute easy spin
- 10 minute warm down

A typical routine for Strength on the spin bike is as follows:
- 10 minute warm up
- 1 minute one leg pedal at 70 rpms (high resistance)
- 2 minute x 120 rpms (low resistance)
- Repeat using other leg.
- Alternate between legs for a total of 10 times per leg.
- 10 minute warm down.

A typical routine for Speed Training on the velodrome behind a motor is as follows:
- 20 minute warm up
- Roll off the banking to 200 meter line
- Flying 200 meter behind motor – 3 to 5 reps
- 15 to 20 minute recovery
- Gears 82 to 92
- 10 minute warm down in small gear

A typical routine for power training on the velodrome is as follows:
- 20 minute warm up with all out sprint on last lap.
- 5 minute rest or until heart rate recovers
- Change gear to 82" or if that is warm up gear keep it on.
- Standing start 400 meter negative split effort building to 90%
- 3 minute rest or until heart rate recovers
- Repeat this sequence by changing gears to 90, 92, 94, 96, 98, 108
- 10 minute warm down in 82 inch gear

Negative splits means to execute the first half of the event at a slower pace than the second half of the event. The purpose is to finish strong rather than use up all of your energy stores and die at the end. From a standing start - 400 meters should take you about 35 seconds to complete on the velodrome.

A typical routine for Acceleration Training is as follows:
- 20 minute warm up
- 6 seconds standing start sprints – maximal
- Distance 50 to 60 meters
- 2 sets of 5 reps
- Gear 92 – 100
- 5 minutes recovery between rides
- 20 minute recovery between sets
- 10 minute warm down in small gear.

Training analysis for sprint events

Track cycling training programs appear to be highly secretive and what works for one person might not work for you. I have found that Track and Field training for 100 meter and 800 meter events are pretty much similar to the training for Track Cycling flying 200 meter and kilo events. The same energy systems have to be trained therefore the training programs are similar. Training for the kilo pretty much places you in good shape for the flying 200 meters, since both events are essentially sprint events and there is some training overlap. Below is an analysis of times for various events I did. The father of all books regarding Periodization and Training is one called "Periodization" by Tudor Bompa and Gregory Haff. Also it seems that a good sprinter should be able to go farther faster, in other words speed endurance workouts should be focused on.

Best 2009 Kilo time with 200 meter split times:

Best Kilo time 1.19:98 on 8/8/2009 – Kissena Velodrome
Splits
- 200 meter = 19.94 = 19.94 seconds
- 400 meter = 15.55 = 35.49 seconds
- 600 meter = 14.37 = 49.86 seconds
- 800 meter = 14.53 = 64.39 seconds
- 1000 meter = 15.59 = 79.98 seconds = 1.19:98

Gear used 52 x 13 = 108 inch (Gear is too big to get started quickly, looking to go down to a 50 x 14 = 96" or 51 x14 = 98" or 52 x 14 = 100")

Equipment:
- Tiemeyer bike
- Karbona rear disk wheel with 21 mm tufo tubular tire
- Karbona front tri spoke with 19 mm tufo tubular tire
- Tire pressure - 140 psi
- Louis Garneau Rocket aero helmet
- Profile Aero bars
- Long sleeve skinsuit
- Shoe covers

Best 2009 standing 400 meter one lap time:
32.44 seconds on 6/8/2009 - Kissena Velodrome
Gear 50 x 15 = 90"

Equipment:
- Tiemeyer Bike
- Karbona rear disk with 21 mm tufo tubular
- Karbona front tri spoke with 19 mm tufo tubular
- Tire pressure 140 psi
- Louis Garneau rocket aero helmet
- Long sleeve skinsuit
- Shoe covers
- Regular bars

Best 2009 Flying 200 meter time:
12.57 seconds on 8/30/2009 - Kissena Velodrome
Gear 52 x 13 = 108"

Equipment:
- Tiemeyer bike
- Mavic Ellipse clinchers with Vittoria Open Corsa Evo 23 mm tires

- Tire pressure - 140 psi
- Louis Garneau Rocket aero helmet
- Long sleeve skinsuit
- Shoe covers

Best 1600 meter pursuit time:
2.15:51 on 6/8/2009 - Kissena Velodrome
Gear 50 x 15 = 90"

Equipment:
- Tiemeyer Bike
- Karbona rear disk with 21 mm tufo tubular
- Karbona front tri spoke with 19 mm tufo tubular
- Tire pressure 140 psi
- Louis Garneau rocket aero helmet
- Long sleeve skinsuit
- Shoe covers
- Profile aero bars

The strength and power weight-training I am doing, weight used and number of sets, reps and duration of rest:

- Before embarking on a weight training program, it is advised that you should first have a base of functional strength. You must be able to manipulate your body weight by being able to do exercises such as push ups, pull ups, vertical jumps, standing long jumps etc. So I did a base line fit test to check functional strength. It is one thing to be able to lie on your back and do a 200 lb bench press and another to do 100 push ups in one minute. Not too many sports require you to lie on your back and press a weight.

- For strength training I did a one rep max test to determine maximum weight I can lift, based on that I do 4 sets per exercise at the required percentage of weight (6 to 4 reps) increasing the weight on each set and reducing reps, with

79

1 to 2 minutes rest between sets. Main exercises are the half squat with thighs parallel to the floor, hack squat, dead lifts and leg press. Also a lot of unilateral exercises with lighter weights. One particularly functional exercise is to hold a 25 to 45 lb plate in front of you while standing on a box or bench, then squat down on one leg and come back up. This works the core, hips, thighs and balancing muscles. I noticed that body weight went up during this phase of training.

- For hypertrophy training I do 4 sets per exercise (8 to 10 reps) increasing weight on each set and reducing reps with 1 to 2 minute rest between sets. Main exercise is the full squat with butt all the way to the floor.

- For power training, I pick a weight I can handle and do 5 to 8 reps with 2 to 3 minutes rest between sets, increasing the weight slightly with each set and reducing reps. Main exercise is the power clean and the 5x5x5 squat (5 regular squats, 5 squats rising to the toes and 5 squats jumps with 135 lbs on my shoulders). I also do plyometric jumps such as box jumps, unilateral jumps, squat jumps, plyometric push ups. I also wear a 20lb weighted vest for some of these plyometric exercises.

- Before weight training I do a movement prep warm up which focuses on getting the body warmed up for exercise. Movement prep routine includes core work, twisting exercises, push ups, pull ups, sit ups, lunges, dynamic stretching with tension bands, balance moves with physioball. Also, exercises to develop agility and coordination.

Hours of weight training in a typical week:

- Approximately 6 hours.

The kind of spin bike I am using, and a typical spin workout:

- Saris Cyclops 300 PT Pro ($2,000).

- As it gets closer to racing season - Tabata intervals in the mornings three times a week on days I weight train - 20 seconds max effort 10 seconds rest for 8 reps (4 minutes worth of work), five minutes warm up and five minute cool down - wattage range from about 250 to 450 watts. Noticed that since I started interval training, body weight and body fat percentage have gone down.

- Two hour rides at endurance level intensity based off my FTP testing.

- Intervals at Vo2 max threshold 1 min to 8 minutes with one to one work to rest ratio, Vo2 max range based on current FTP test.

- Intervals at Lactate threshold 10 min to 20 minutes with one to one work to rest ratio, lactate range based on current FTP test.

- Recovery rides based on current FTP test.

- Leg speed workouts - spin at 120 to 130 rpms for 5 to 10 minutes and try to max out for about 10 seconds at 190 rpms with very low resistance.

- Sprint and standing start workouts with heavy resistance, 5 to 30 seconds sprints.

Hours of spinning in a typical week:

- Approximately 6 hours.

Duration, volume and intensity I was averaging for the last month:

- Typical duration of spin bike workout is 1 hour

- Distance about 20 miles for 1 hour.

- Depending on the intensity then the work done would range from about 150 to 500 Kj of work for 1 hour.

Functional Threshold Power (FTP) test to see if my base has been optimized and power output maximized. These are the numbers as of February 2010:

- I do a 20 minute FTP test on the spin bike using the protocol from Training and Racing with a Power Meter by Hunter, Allen; & Coogan, Andrew.

What do I use to measure load (work):

- Both heart rate and power meter.

- On the Cyclops 300 PT Pro spin bike I use their wireless module to measure heart and power – power takes precedence over heart rate when I am training with power since cardiac drift causes the heart rate to rise even though the perceived exertion is the same. Power is an absolute value and a true reflection of your output and work.

- On the road and track I use a Garmin Edge 305 GPS to record and measure heart rate, speed, distance, profiles. There is no power capability to measure power here.

- At the Gym or at home doing P90X workouts I use a Garmin pulse watch to record and measure heart rate.

Current resting heart rate:

- 59 bpm

Current maximum heart rate:

- 186 bpm

My power output at anaerobic threshold (Lactate Threshold):

- Current power output at anaerobic threshold (Lactate Threshold) is about 210 to 222 watts, March 2010

- Current 30 second sprint power is 1,195 watts with an average of 750 watts, March 2010

- Current 10 second sprint power is 1,212 watts, March 2010

- Age 45
- Weight 172 lbs
- Fat 15%
- Height 5'-9"

Neuromuscular Adaptation

I have noticed my flying 200 meter times are faster after about 5 or 6 - 100% efforts in warm up gears and then at least one effort in the race gear, providing I get full recovery between efforts. There is no doubt the time spent warming up will improve performance, but I found it important to also do a 100% effort in my race gear. This allows the brain, nervous system and muscles to get synchronized to the action and line needed to do my best flying 200 meter. So don't expect to do your best time on your first effort in race gear.

Leg Speed

suggestion is to teach the body to do what you want it to
\[t\]his is what exercise physiologists call "motor
\[pr\]ogramming." The body tends to remember its last effort and
looks back to that "map" for instructions on what it should do the
next time you call on it. So let's take advantage of this
phenomenon, by tricking it and training it.

That is why five minutes of high-cadence pedaling in the small
ring before and after big-gear/low-cadence stuff. This primes the
neuromuscular system before the effort and reprograms it
afterwards, helping it to remember "fast." It also serves to help
clear the legs of any metabolic waste.

To really take this to the next level, let's do the same thing in the
gym, where it may have an even greater impact. Try working in
three to five minutes of 100 to 110+ rpm pedaling on the
stationary bike before your weight-training sessions to wake up
the neuromuscular system, and especially after your workout to
retrain it after you lift.

Optimal Cadence Range
I read in the US Cycling manual, that a track cyclist should be
able to maintain about 133 rpms for a duration of 7 minutes in a
typical endurance race gear.

As we get older, cardiovascular capacity slowly diminishes.
Keeping in mind the goal of deriving one's potential should be
placed on pacing strategies, cadence and gear selection. Optimal
cadence is a trade-off between cycling economy, power output
and the development of fatigue.

For me to achieve my times in the Kilo and Flying 200 meter,
then I would have to increase my cadence range to between 110 -
125 rpms. Also depending on the distance of the event I would
then have to pick the right gear which would allow me to achieve
this average cadence range.

For the Flying 200 meter it would have to be a gear between a 98" to 108" depending on the line I take, type of track and weather conditions.

For the Kilo it would have to be a gear between 92 to 96 depending on type of track and weather conditions.

Motor Pacing
- The scooter/motorcycle should be able to go up to 70 km/hr (45 mph)

- Anything much more than an 80-100cc scooter may be too powerful and accelerate too quickly at the higher speeds for the riders behind to keep up with. The small increases in speed may not seem like much to the driver, but 2 or 3 mph/hr is a big deal to the cyclists on the back who are on hanging on for dear life.

- Ideally you want a roller on back of the scooter. Keep an eye out for any protrusions that could catch a wheel at the ends of roller.

- The motorcycle should have an extended mirror so that the driver can see predetermined hand signals.

- Give the hand signals between the driver and riders some serious thought and spend time understanding them. The driver will NOT be able to hear the riders and will be looking for visual cues in his mirror. This is #1 for safety. Establish signals for slow down, speed up, sprint, etc. as well as safety signals.

- The motorcycles should have a lowered exhaust so the riders behind aren't breathing in fumes for hours on end.

- More than 4 or 5 riders on a motorpacing session gets to be too many. The further back the rider is from the motorbike, the harder it gets because there is less of a draft. Right behind the motorbike is the area where you get the most rest (relatively speaking). The riders behind are doing the most work.

- Don't just go out and motorpace without some proper strength and power blocks of training. If you do this you'll gain some form for a while, but you won't have the underlying fitness to keep it going and build upon it.

- Make sure that you motorpace after you have a good base of strength and you'll be able to push the bigger gears faster. Use motorpacing as "top up" training about a month out from when you want to reach your peak.

- The training effect that motorpacing has on the riders is speed. The neuromuscular training effect associated with being in the draft and using higher leg speed (less torque) will help you increase the speed component of your training. It also improves the psychological element of not being completely in control of pace (similar to a race – this is where a good motorpace driver who knows you makes a big difference)

- If the cyclist behind the bike separates as little as 1 ft off of the rear of the motorbike, the workload will spike incredibly high to regain the "sweet spot" of the draft that is best only inches away from the bumper. Once or twice and this isn't an issue, but after an hour of motorpacing which is usually done in zone 4/5, that wattage spike really hurts.

Track cycling drills
There are numerous combination of drills which can be created and done on the track to train various energy systems. Below are a few.

Taking laps:
Riders are instructed to ride in a single file manner at a steady
pace, riders should use this as a warm up to the exercise and
recovery phase during the exercise.

Once the riders are settled into formation the exercise can begin,
a rider at the front will launch up to speed by dropping down the
velodrome banking accelerating to the white line at the bottom of
the track using the shortest route to get around and gain a lap on
the rest of the group who are cruising at a normal pace.

It is important for the riders when rejoining the group to scrub
off their speed by riding up over the top of the tail end of the
group, this helps them to slow the track bike down without
having to back pedal to reduce speed, also from the safety point
of view the track beneath the group is clear for the lead rider or
riders to drop down when it is the next riders turn to launch off
the front.

Russian sprints
These are used for anaerobic conditioning (speed endurance)
where you have four riders in race gears or over geared riding for
two laps. On the first lap you start at the top of the banking while
the speed is ramped up incrementally to about 90%, the first and
third rider will then peel off at the 200 meter line leaving the
second and fourth rider to sprint all out for the finish line. The
fourth rider is the one who will have to work the hardest to close
the gap on the second rider and try to come around. This is
similar to being motor paced for sprint efforts.

Staggered sprints
This is another form of anaerobic conditioning where two riders
in various gears will ride for two laps starting at the top of the
banking and then drop down to the bottom while incrementally
ramping up the speed to 90% while heading for the finish line.
The rider in the back would usually ride a smaller gear than the

rider in the front whereby having to work harder to keep up with the rider in the front.

Cog sprints to improve strength
Roll onto the track in the sprinters lane. Move up to the outside of the sprinters lane when coming out of the final bend. Keep rolling and increase the speed slightly while still in the saddle. Get out of the saddle and kick hard when approaching the pursuit line. Pedal hard and keep on going in a line that goes to the top of the embankment. One should reach the top of the embankment at the middle portion of the bend. Start coasting when at the top of the embankment and ride down and back into the sprinters lane. Keep rolling through the back straight and the next bend before preparing for the next sprint. Repeat 15 times. An alternative and tougher workout is to repeat the cog sprint at both bends. Repeat 15 times.

Tip: Some track efforts such as sprints and standing starts can be practiced in a closed parking lot or artificial turf / grass playing field if you live far from the track.

Fig 31: Rider warming up at Kissena

Chapter 6 – Weight Training

Functional Training
We move in patterns, and muscles work together. So you have to train your muscles and nervous system to work in complete patterns and not in isolation. You have to train your body to build strength while still being athletic. Compound movements will do this, free weight squats and deadlifts are examples of compound movements. Stay away from body building isolation type exercises, you need to build functional strength. P90X by Beachbody is a great structured off season work out program to build functional strength and to lose body fat.

As resistance training becomes more accepted by endurance athletes, coaches and conditioning specialists are seeking dynamic training programs to prescribe to their athletes. Functional training can provide a unique challenge that benefits all aspects of athletic performance as well as offering an enjoyable supplement to traditional resistance training.

Functional training is defined as "training for a specific purpose or duty" by Juan Santana, one of the most respected strength and conditioning specialists. The concept of function varies from activity to activity and from individual to individual, thus encompassing a wide spectrum of activities. What is functional for one group of individuals may not be functional for others. For example, training strategies for strength and power sports may not be functional for endurance athletes, and the training program for an elite cyclist will not be functional for the beginning rider.

Functional training should address the unique concerns that face all athletes:

- Potential for overuse injuries due to the training volume necessary for success
- Strength and flexibility imbalances

- Inevitable neuromuscular fatigue that can hamper the performance of virtually every athlete. --Core strength weaknesses that diminish the efficient force production between the upper and lower extremities.

Functional training programs and exercises should involve integrated activities that demand balance and coordination to enhance proprioception (joint awareness). The methods and equipment used for these dynamic exercises hold several advantages over traditional or machine-based resistance training. First, these activities require that the athlete create his or her own stability necessary for the exercise rather than relying on a machine or bench to provide the stability.

Fig 32: Rider resting after a hard effort at Kissena

Using tools to enhance balance and stability recruits often-neglected stabilizer muscles, which may result in fewer overuse-type injuries. This concept is referred to as pre-habilitation - realizing that a potential for injury exists and the specific prevention strategies implemented to prevent such occurrences.

Bodyweight: A fundamental element to functional training is for the athlete to develop control over one's body before attempting to externally load an exercise or movement. Using body weight exercises forces the athlete to focus on balance and dynamic stabilization during the movement. Examples of excellent bodyweight exercises include push-ups, pull-ups, dips, squats, lunges, split squats and step-ups. Best of all, no equipment is required and these exercises can be performed virtually anytime and anywhere.

Competition Tapering:
You've trained hard, prepared well, got your weight down, power up and you are as fit as you've been all year. Your key event is just around the corner; so what now? When is enough, enough? When is too much, too much? And when's the right time to throttle back to be mentally and physically fresh for your big day?

What is a taper?
A taper is considered to be a period of time where the volume of training is reduced in the days or weeks leading up to a key event to prevent training-induced fatigue from impacting your performance on the day. It isn't done for every event just the one or two a year that you have pre-determined to be your key objectives for peak performance. The key to a well executed taper period is finding the best balance between recovery and sustained training.

A structured taper will allow the body to recover from the accumulated fatigue of hard training without reversing the affects of training adaptation. The best training and form in the world can all be wasted with an ineffective taper period. Get it right and you'll fly on the day, get it wrong and you'll not be competing to your full potential

Tabata intervals:

This is an example of a work to rest interval protocol used during a taper, 20 seconds of 100% effort with 10 seconds of rest and repeated 8 times, by the 4th rep you will be at your anaerobic threshold if done properly since you are not getting enough rest to fully recover. Your work to rest ratio is 2 to 1 and this will really stress your body.

Fig 33: A junior rider sitting on the wheel of a seasoned rider at Kissena

Type of weight Training:
Based on the One Rep Max (RM), I am doing a combination of Medium to Low intensity workouts alternating between upper body on one day and lower body another day. This gives the muscles 72 hours to recover and repair.

My one rep Max (1RM) for Squat and Bench Press.

Exercise	1RM	90%	80%	70%	60%	50%	40%
Squat	325lbs	292lbs	260lbs	227lbs	195lbs	162lbs	**130lbs**
Bench	235lbs	211lbs	188lbs	164lbs	141lbs	**117lbs**	94lbs

Currently doing a combination of Hypertrophy / Endurance weight training using relatively light weights.

Variable	Strength	Power	Hypertrophy	Endurance
% of 1 RM	80 to 90	45 to 55	**60 to 80**	**40 to 60**
Reps per set	1 to 5	1 to 5	**6 to 12**	**15 to 60**
Sets	4 to 7	3 to 5	**4 to 6**	**2 to 4**
Rest bet sets (mins)	2 to 6	2 to 6	**2 to 5**	**1 to 2**
Time per set (secs)	5 to 10	4 to 8	**20 to 60**	**80 to 150**

Intensity, Volume & Frequency

Variable	High	Med	Low
Intensity(% 1RM)	80 to 90%	**50 to 80%**	10 to 40%
Volume per muscle	1 exercise	**2 exercises**	3 + exercises
Sets	1 set	**2 – 3 sets**	4 + sets
Reps	1 – 6 reps	**8 – 15 reps**	20 + reps
Session Frequency	1 per week	**2 – 3 per week**	4 + per week

Warm up & Core before weight training

Exercise	Set 1	Set 2	Set 3
Back stretch	8 reps	8 reps	
Groin stretch	8 reps		
One leg balance	8 reps		
Hamstring stretch	8 reps		
Hamstring curl	8 reps		
Core crunch	8 reps		
Crunches	20 reps		
Leg raises	10 reps	10 reps	10 reps
Jump Squats	10 reps	10 reps	10 reps

Chapter 7 – Plyometrics

Plyometrics is a type of exercise training designed to produce fast, powerful movements, and improve the functions of the nervous system, generally for the purpose of improving performance in a specific sport. Plyometric movements, in which a muscle is loaded and then contracted in rapid sequence using the strength and elasticity of a muscle and its surrounding tissues to jump higher, run faster, throw farther, or hit harder, depending on the desired training goal. Plyometrics is used to increase the speed or force of muscular contractions, often with the goal of increasing the height of a jump.

Plyometric training involves practicing plyometric movements to toughen tissues and train nerve cells to stimulate a specific pattern of muscle contraction so the muscle generates as strong a contraction as possible in the shortest amount of time. A plyometric contraction involves first a rapid muscle lengthening movement, followed by a short resting phase, then an explosive muscle shortening movement, which enables muscles to work together in doing the particular motion. Plyometric training engages the myostatic-reflex, which is the automatic contraction of muscle when their stretch nerve receptors are stimulated.

Plyometric exercises use explosive movements to develop muscular power, the ability to generate a large amount of force quickly. Plyometric training acts on the nerves, muscles, and tendons to increase an athlete's power output without necessarily increasing their maximum strength.

Muscular power is determined by how long it takes for strength to be converted into speed. The ability to convert strength to speed in a very short time allows for athletic movements beyond what raw strength will allow. Thus an athlete who has strong legs and can perform the free weight squat with extremely heavy weights over a long duration may get less distance on a standing long jump or height on a vertical leap than a weaker athlete who is able to generate a smaller amount of force but in a shorter amount of time. The plyometrically trained athlete may have a lower maximal force output, and thus may not squat as much, but his training allows him to shorten the amount of time required to reach his maximum force output, leading to more power from each contraction.

Fig 34: Rider celebrating his victories at Kissena

For a muscle to cause movement, it must shorten; this is known as a concentric contraction. There is a maximum amount of force with which a certain muscle can concentrically contract. However, if the muscle is lengthened while loaded (eccentric contraction) just prior to the contraction, it will produce greater force through the storage of elastic energy. This effect requires that the transition time between eccentric contraction and concentric contraction (amortization phase) be very short. This energy dissipates rapidly, so the concentric contraction must rapidly follow the eccentric stretch. The process is frequently referred to as the "stretch shortening cycle", and is one of the underlying mechanisms of plyometric training. Usually after plyometric exercise the tendon stretches and the thighs and quadriceps feel tender.

In addition to the elastic-recoil of the musculotendonous system there is a neurological component. The stretch shortening cycle affects the sensory response of the muscle spindles and golgi tendon organs (GTO). It is believed that during plyometric exercise, the excitatory threshold of the GTO's is increased, making them less likely to send signals to limit force production when the muscle has increased tension. This facilitates greater contraction force than normal strength or power exercise, and thus greater training ability.

The muscle spindles are involved in the stretch reflex and are triggered by rapid lengthening of the muscle as well as absolute length. At the end of the rapid eccentric contraction, the muscle has reached a great length at a high velocity. This may cause the muscle spindle to enact a powerful stretch reflex, further enhancing the power of the following concentric contraction. The muscle spindle's sensitivity to velocity is another reason why the amortization phase must be brief for a plyometric effect.

Plyometric exercises involve an increased risk of injury due to the large forces generated during training and performance, and should only be performed by well-conditioned individuals who are under supervision. Good levels of physical strength, flexibility and proprioception should be achieved before commencement of plyometric training.

The specified minimum strength requirement varies depending on where the information is sourced and the intensity of the plyometrics to be performed. Chu (1998) recommends that a participant be able to perform 5 repetitions of the squat exercise at 60% of their bodyweight before doing plyometrics. Core body (trunk) strength is also important.

Flexibility is required both for injury prevention and to enhance the effect of the stretch shortening cycle.

Proprioception is an important component of balance, coordination and agility, which are also required for safe performance of plyometric exercises.

Further safety considerations include:

- Age - low-intensity and low-volume only for athletes under the age of 13 or for athletes who squat less than 1.5 times their bodyweight.

- Surface - some degree of softness is needed. Gymnastics mats are ideal, grass is suitable. Hard surfaces such as concrete should never be used.

- Bodyweight - athletes who are over 240 pounds (109 kg) should be very careful and low-intensity plyometric exercises should be selected.

- Technique - most importantly, a participant must be instructed on proper technique before commencing any plyometric exercise. They should be well rested and free of injury in any of the limbs to be exercised.

- Plyometrics is not inherently dangerous, but the highly focused, intense movements used in repetition increase the potential level of stress on joints and musculo-tendonous units. Therefore safety precautions are a strong prerequisite to this particular method of exercise. Low-intensity variations of plyometrics are frequently utilized in various stages of injury rehabilitation, indicating that the application of proper technique and appropriate safety precautions can make plyometric safe and effective for most populations.

Reference: Wikipedia

P90X .
The P90X exercise system is a great off season fitness program to get your body in shape for rigorous activities. It is like having a personal trainer in your living room with the use of minimal equipment. I found the Plyometric training is the most intense workout in this program. You need to be in reasonable shape to start the P90X fitness program. Getting fit the P90X way means working out 6-7 days per week, with each workout lasting about 1-1½ hours.

The P90X program cost about $119, this is a bargain as compared to the exorbitant cost of gym memberships, coaches and cycling equipment. This program is great value for the money and you get a lot of utility out of it with quantifiable results. The program comes with 12 workout DVDs, a 100-page fitness guide, a 113-page nutrition plan, and a 90-day calendar to track your progress. (You'll need some additional equipment -- a pull-up bar, dumbbells, resistance bands, and an exercise mat.) You can do your own research online and read the reviews of the program and make your own decision. It is a good program that encompasses all the training and nutrition protocols needed to get fit and lean. It is also structured in a logical building block manner.

Each workout is presented in a circuit format, in which you move from exercise to exercise with little rest in between, thus keeping your heart rate up. The strengthening DVDs target certain parts of the body each day: chest and back; then shoulders and arms; legs and back; chest, shoulders, and triceps; and back and biceps.

Other DVDs focus on Plyometrics, Kenpo kickboxing, Cardio fitness, Abs/Core, Yoga, and Stretching.

For example, the "Chest & Back" DVD is a 53-minute workout that works the chest muscles with variations of the push-up, including traditional push-ups, wide-stance "fly" push-ups, and push-ups done with your hands close together. It targets the back muscles with variations of the pull-up or pull-down exercise done with resistance bands, including pull-ups/pull-downs with your hands at shoulder width, wider, narrower, or reverse grip. It also includes rowing exercises done with dumbbells or resistance bands.

The 60-minute "Plyometrics" workout is the most intense in the P90X system. After a lengthy warm-up, this cardiovascular routine leads you through a series of jumping moves that primarily work the lower body to build explosive repeatable power.

The P90X system is based on the concept of "muscle confusion," which means varying the workout schedule and introducing new moves so the body never fully adapts. This is similar to the periodization techniques as described earlier. It also has a basis in science; research suggests that workout programs that offer variation bring greater benefits than those that do not.

What this means is that over the 90-days of the P90X program, you'll change your weekly workout schedule every 3-4 weeks. You can also tailor your routine to the kind of results you want

The classic P90X program involves 13 weeks of alternating the three following weekly routines.

Weeks 1-3, and weeks 9 and 11:

- Day 1: Chest & Back and 16-minute Ab Ripper DVD
- Day 2: Plyometrics
- Day 3: Shoulders & Arms and Ab Ripper

- Day 4: Yoga
- Day 5: Legs & Back and Ab Ripper
- Day 6: Kenpo
- Day 7: Rest, or Stretching workout

Weeks 5-7, and weeks 10 and 12:

- Day 1: Chest, Shoulders, and Triceps; Ab Ripper
- Day 2: Plyometrics
- Day 3: Back & Biceps, Ab Ripper
- Day 4: Yoga
- Day 5: Legs & Back, Ab Ripper
- Day 6: Kenpo
- Day 7: Rest or Stretching workout

Weeks 4, 8, and 13:

- Day 1: Yoga
- Day 2: Core Synergistics
- Day 3: Kenpo
- Day 4: Stretch
- Day 5: Core Synergistics
- Day 6: Yoga
- Day 7: Rest or Stretching workout

The P90X nutrition plan that accompanies the fitness DVDs has three phases you can follow at any time, based on your current fitness and nutrition level:

- Phase 1, the "Fat Shredder," is a diet high in protein and low in carbohydrates and fat.
- Phase 2, "Energy Booster," calls for a more balanced mix of protein and carbohydrates, along with a small amount of fat.
- Phase 3,""Endurance Maximizer," has higher levels of complex carbs, a moderate amount of protein, and a small amount of fat.

If you're already fairly fit, the P90X system is an excellent workout for losing body fat and increasing muscle tone. The P90X workouts are designed for healthy people in good physical condition. In addition to the cost for the P90X system, you'll need to buy some basic resistance training equipment if you don't already have it (5 to 30 lb dumbbell weights, bands, pull-up bar and mat). The P90X workout DVDs are mainly geared toward improving muscular endurance, muscle tone, and cardiovascular fitness which is the backbone of racing a bicycle.

The circuits target one body part right after another, which is great for a muscle-pumping/toning workout, but not ideal for increasing strength. For optimum development of muscle strength and size, it's recommended that you rest at least 1 minute between each set to fully recover so you can lift maximum weight on the next set.

The P90X workout system is simple - just follow the program for 90 days and you'll be more muscular and leaner than you ever imagined. But these challenging workouts require lots of dedication to complete. I started the program at 184 lbs after not racing my bicycle for a year, after 90 days I was a lean 165 lbs – see before and after photo below. I was also able to produce more wattage during my FTP test at a lower body weight and heart rate, which is the goal of any training program.

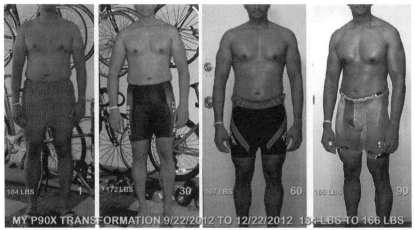

Fig 35: My before and after transformation using P90X –
progress pictures taken every 30 days.

Fig 36: 1970 Labor Day meet at Kissena – photo provided by
Debbie & Larry DeSario

Chapter 8 – Weight Management

Over the past five years, I tried various programs to lose fat. The one that was promising was the P90X fitness program. I took the year off from riding and racing my bicycle in 2012 and my weight ballooned up from 172 lbs to 184 lbs even though I still continued lifting weights in the gym four days per week, I got stronger and bigger. Most of the weight I put on was fat since I did not follow a restricted calorie diet. I decided to go on a program to lose fat not muscle, I therefore cut most sugars, restricted the carbohydrates, maintained the protein intake and upped the intensity of my workouts. I restricted myself to 1800 calories for the first two weeks to get my body moving in the fat burning direction - I then upped the calories to 2400 calories. I also drank a lot of water to flush the system and to help metabolize the fats – no sodas, no fruit juices and no beer or alcohol.

Fig 37: Rider cruising around Kissena

I worked out first thing in the morning before breakfast for one hour. Your body has enough glycogen stored up for an hour of intense workout it also uses the fat stores for energy since carbohydrates are not available. Working out in the morning will boost your metabolism for the next two days, I noticed a drop in weight two days later. Then the weight would rise slightly the next day then drop even lower the following day. Weight loss is not linear it is more of a step down. I was losing about 1 pound of fat every week on the P90X program. The type of workout I did was based on the circuit training or interval protocol, where you would move from one exercise to another with minimal to no rest, this creates the intensity needed to burn fat and lose weight. One hour of this type of workout burns about 700 calories. I went from 184 lbs to 165 lbs of relatively lean muscle mass in 90 days. I was down to my target weight of 165 lbs in 90 days, but you have to put in the work and you have to be disciplined enough to follow the diet guide lines by cutting out all the junk foods, excess carbohydrates and sugars. Unfortunately we haven't reached the point where we can buy the type of body or health we want in stores or on Amazon as yet. It is extremely hard to stay lean on an American diet, since the foods are highly processed with too many preservatives and sugar. The food pyramid is designed based on economics and not health benefits. It has also become very expensive to eat healthy unprocessed foods. It is what you call the progress trap, where countries progress to the point where they can genetically alter their food supply with no real health benefits except economic and whereby processed and genetically altered foods become cheaper than the healthier naturally grown organic foods.

My body fat percentage went down, but this number varies depending on the method used to measure it. My body fat percentage is somewhere between 10 % and 15 % which is still too high for an endurance athlete. There still remains some fat around the lower abdominals which will take a little longer to get rid of, if a strict diet is followed. Body fat percentage varies depending on the method used for measuring it, I believe the most accurate measurement is the water displacement method found in Universities, other than that the caliper method is probably the most accurate.

What is the point of taking part in competitive sports such as bicycle racing when you carry around excess body fat and are not able to keep up with younger leaner athletes? I fell into the trap, thinking that better equipment would make up for the difference. But much more benefits could be derived at a cheaper cost if you were to get your body where it should be, a leaner body is more aerodynamic and power to weight ratio increases when you are not carrying around excess body fat. It is no wonder that skinny teens and 20 year olds are able to ride rings around older heavier athletes.

The equipment I used was a pull up bar in the doorway. Five sets of dumbbells ranging from 30, 25, 15, 10 and 5 lbs and a pair of push up bars. I used a heart rate monitor to record some of the workouts to get an idea of intensity and caloric expenditure. By day 13 my resting pulse went from mid 70s to mid to lower 60s in the morning and at night before bed it was in the mid 50s. One thing to note is that your last meal for the day should be 3 hours before bedtime to allow for it to digest properly. You don't want to go to bed on a full stomach which will turn to fat. That was my problem before when I worked out at the gym in the evenings and got home late to eat. I therefore switched to working out in the mornings on an empty stomach with only a glass of water before the workout to help metabolize the fats. The first two weeks of the program were the hardest since the carbs were restricted and calories were restricted, I suffered withdrawal symptoms or what they call the 'Carb Flu'. P90X is not a muscle building hypertrophy program, it is more of a weight loss and cardiovascular fitness program based on circuit training. To build muscle you need more rest between sets and do less reps using heavier weights, this program does not allow for that.

Caloric expenditure for each individual workout for 7 days:

1. Chest and back, abdominals 77 minutes-**1,052**
2. Plyometrics 60 mins-**871**
3. Shoulder biceps triceps, abdominals 60 minutes-**961**

4. Yoga 92 minutes-**809**
5. Legs/back 60 minutes-**865**
6. Kenpo 60 minutes-**688**
7. Stretch 60 minutes-**303**
   - **Total Calories 5,549**
   - Total time 485 minutes or 8 hours
   - **Average Calories per hour was 693 per workout for seven days.**

Metrics for the 90 day workout:
Below is an order of magnitude estimate for the total amount of movement reps of exercises during the 12 weeks of workout and the total amount of cumulative dumbbell weights lifted. Reps times weight gives the total amount of weight lifted during that week. Also below is an estimate of caloric expenditure during the 90 days.

Total calories consumed during the program would be about **2200 calories per day** x 90 days = **198,000 calories.**

Total calories burnt during the program would be about **650 calories per day** x 90 days = **58,500 calories.** I worked out seven days were week.

Total weight lifted during 90 days was **27,129 lbs** divide by **2240 lbs** = **12.1 Tons**

.

Total movement	**39,942 reps**	
Total push ups	**2,200 reps**	
Total pull ups	**700 reps**	
Total Sit ups	**15,000 reps**	
	Movements	**Weight**
Week 1	1389 reps	375 lbs
Week 2	1311 reps	810 lbs
Week 3	1305 reps	570 lbs
Week 4	recovery	week

107

Week 5	2425 reps	2972 lbs
Week 6	3585 reps	3597 lbs
Week 7	4387 reps	4182 lbs
Week 8	recovery	week
Week 9	5204 reps	5984 lbs
Week 10	5947 reps	6539 lbs
Week 11	6815 reps	755 lbs
Week 12	7574 reps	1345 lbs
Totals	**39,942 reps**	**27,129 lbs**

As you can see the intensity increased as the weeks went by, just by looking at the amount of movement reps and pounds lifted. There is a great App for the iPhone from P90X that helps you keep track of your workout progress and calories based on portion sizes.

Fig 38: 1982 Labor Day meet at Kissena – photo provided by Debbie & Larry DeSario

Chapter 9 – Nutrition and Supplements

Supplements and advertising hype! I couldn't really say if they work or not. It is not like you feel the effects immediately like Popeye consuming a can of spinach. The only supplement where I noticed a reaction, is Creatine Monohydrate - it gives me head aches and leaves me feeling bloated. Maybe they work and maybe they don't, I guess you can get the same benefits from a proper diet. A good documentary to watch which gives you the inside scoop and scams on supplements is "Bigger Stronger Faster". Imagine some folks in Utah were filling capsules with flour and using slick marketing techniques to market the product as the next big muscle growth formula, using before and after pictures which were shot the same day and retouched in Adobe Photoshop. Below is a list of supplements with marketing hype obtained from the web. Have you ever watched the news and they report the benefits of coffee, and a couple of weeks later they report that coffee is harmful to you - depending on the sponsors of the newscast? That is the same way supplements come across, it is a confusing hodge podge of information thrown at you. I don't know if these supplements work or not, all I know is that a lot of money is spent to advertise supplements.

First Endurance Optygen: The two main adaptogens in Optygen were first used by Tibetan Sherpas to help them climb Mount Everest. Optygen utilizes these unique adaptogens because clinical research (on elite endurance athletes) has shown them to increase oxygen utilization. This increases the body's ability to adapt to high levels of physical stress, increase anaerobic threshold and reduce lactic acid.

Endurox Excel: Endurox is a natural dietary supplement that when taken as part of a normal workout regimen can increase fat metabolism and improve workout performance. Endurox is a pure standardized extract of the herb ciwujia (su wah ja). Ciwujia, a root grown in the northeast section of China, has been used safely in Traditional Chinese Medicine for almost 1700 years to treat fatigue and bolster the immune system. Ciwujia has also been used by mountain climbers to improve performance at high altitudes.

Omega 3-6-9: The Omega 3, 6 and 9 groups of fatty acids all contain essential fatty acids necessary for good health. The difference between them lies in the position of the first double bond from the methyl end or the Omega end of the carbon chain. As its name implies, the Omega 3 fatty acids have their first double bond at the 3rd position from the end of the chain, and likewise with the other two. Omega 6 has its first double bond at the 6th position from the end and Omega 9 has it at the 9th position from the end of the chain.

L-Carnitine Liquid: Carnitine, also known as L-carnitine (levocarnitine) is a quaternary ammonium compound synthesized from the amino acids lysine and methionine primarily in the liver and kidneys. It helps in the consumption and disposal of fat in the body because it is responsible for the transport of fatty acids from the cytosol into the mitochondria. It is often sold as a nutritional supplement.

Multivitamin: A multivitamin is a preparation intended to supplement a human diet with vitamins, dietary minerals and other nutritional elements. Such preparations are available in the form of tablets, capsules, pastilles, powders, liquids and injectable formulations.

Vitamin C: Vitamin C or L-ascorbic acid is an essential nutrient for humans, a large number of higher primate species, a small number of other mammalian species (notably guinea pigs and bats), a few species of birds, and some fish.

Nitric Oxide: Summary Research papers continue to flood the scientific journals with insights into the biological activity and potential clinical uses of nitric oxide (NO): a gas controlling a seemingly limitless range of functions in the body. Each revelation adds to nitric oxide's already lengthy resume in controlling the circulation of the blood, and regulating activities of the brain, lungs, liver, kidneys, stomach, gut, genitals and other organs.

B-Complex 50: The B-complex vitamins fall into the water-soluble group of vitamins and therefore need to be replenished on a daily basis. They are involved in an extremely large number of important metabolic functions in the human body, including energy production, interconversion of substances, detoxification, nerve transmission, blood formation, synthesis of proteins and fats, the production of steroid hormones, the maintenance of blood sugar levels and appetite, the toning of muscles, etc.

L-Glutamine Powder: L-Glutamine is the most abundant amino acid found in the skeletal muscle. Supplementing with L-Glutamine powder has been clinically proven to aid muscle recovery and energy repletion.

Zinc Magnesium Aspartate: ZMA is a scientifically designed anabolic mineral formula.* It contains Zinc Monomethionine Aspartate plus Magnesium Aspartate and vitamin B-6, and is an all-natural product that clinical testing suggests may significantly increase anabolic hormone levels and muscle strength in trained athletes.

BCAA Powder: Among the most beneficial and effective supplements in any sports nutrition program are branched chain amino acids. These are the essential aminos leucine, isoleucine, and valine.Although these supplements have been around for a long time and the scientific understanding in the exercise performance benefits of BCAA supplementation is rich many people don't know exactly how they exert their effects or how and when to use them properly.

Creatine Monohydrate: So, what is creatine? Our bodies naturally make the compound, which is used to supply energy to our muscles. It is produced in the liver, pancreas, and kidneys, and is transported to the body's muscles through the bloodstream. Once it reaches the muscles, it is converted into phosphocreatine

(creatine phosphate). This high-powered metabolite is used to regenerate the muscles' ultimate energy source, ATP (adenosine triphosphate).

PowerBar Endurance: Powerbar Endurance Sport Drink is a great tasting lemon-lime drink mix for ideal hydration and muscle fuelling to help extend endurance. Studies show that consuming an optimal ratio of glucose and fructose sources regularly during exercise can increase the amounts of carbohydrates that can be digested, delivered to and used by working muscles during exercise by 20-55%. PowerBar Endurance Sports drink now contains C2 MAX, the same optimized ratio of glucose and fructose to help deliver more energy when you need it most.

PowerBar Recovery: Designed to decrease the downtime. Light, refreshing orange flavors create an irresistible "drive to drink". Carbs, Protein and electrolytes ideally formulated for rapid recovery

Muscle Milk Protein Powder: Muscle Milk is not actually milk, or milk derived from muscles. It is a protein powder formulated for the serious athlete or weight lifter. Protein powder is a pure source of protein formulated with lots of vitamins, minerals and without the extra calories and fat. A good protein powder is probably the best muscle-building tool you can buy.

Glyco Maize / Waxy Maize: Waxy maize carbohydrate matrix. 35 g Carbs. 35 mg Carbogen, 50 Servings. The bigger picture of carbohydrates. Whereas proteins help with muscle rebuilding, carbs refuel and replenish. Of the various types available, Waxy Maize Starch and Trehalose are two of the best. Waxy maize starches are long-chain, highly branched, exceptionally-dense complex carbohydrates that are rapidly absorbed. Trehalose is a much smaller, slower-digesting molecule comprised of two unusually linked glucose sugars. Together, these carbohydrates provide immediate and intermediate energy, top-off glycogen stores, and aid with nutrient absorption. That's why they're the foundation of our Glycomaize formula.

Clif Bar: It's the first bar we made, and it's still everything we're about. Whole, all-natural, organic ingredients. Good nutrition. And great taste. Whether you're on a 150-mile bike ride or making your way through a long day, it's the energy bar for everyone.

Power Bar Gel: Refuel with POWERBAR® Gel, featuring POWERBAR® C2 MAX-optimized carbohydrate blend formulated with the same ratio of carb sources shown to increase endurance performance by an average of 8% in 8 trained athletes compared to glucose alone*. During strenuous exercise the body burns carbs and loses key electrolytes through sweat. POWERBAR GEL replenishes and restores those nutrients to help maintain peak performance. For best results,

GU Energy Gel: GU sports energy gel is a favorite of triathletes, cyclists, runners and adventure racers, and endurance athletes everywhere. Used to energize you during exercise, GU energy gel increases endurance during exercise by providing your body with an energy source that helps you keep your energy stable and provides essential electrolytes that help hydrate and balance the body.

Accelerade: Accelerade from Pacific Health Labs is the first endurance sports drink that shifts the energy dynamic during exercise to improve performance. Like conventional sports drinks, Accelerade supplies the necessary carbohydrates and electrolytes for rehydrating and replenishing muscle reserves.But unlike conventional sports and energy drinks, Accelerade has the patented 4 to 1 ratio of carbohydrate to protein to speed the movement of carbohydrate into the muscle. Taken during exercise, Accelerade contains the ideal combination of simple and complex carbohydrates for rapid and sustained energy. By increasing the energy efficiency of every gram of carbohydrate, Accelerade conserves muscle glycogen and improves endurance. Studies show that, compared to a conventional sports drink,

Accelerade extends endurance by 24%. And because Accelerade contains essential antioxidants, it reduces post-exercise muscle damage. Accelerade lets you train longer and harder, and you'll feel less sore afterwards.

Gatorade: Gatorade is a brand of flavored non-carbonated sports drinks manufactured by the Quaker Oats Company, now a division of PepsiCo. Intended for consumption during physically active occasions, Gatorade beverages are formulated to rehydrate and replenish fluid, carbohydrates and electrolytes.

Water: Water is a ubiquitous chemical substance that is composed of hydrogen and oxygen and is essential for all forms of life. Probably the best supplement there is and the reason why this free substance is now being bottled and sold to us under various catchy names as Smart Water, Artisian Water, Polar Spring Water, etc.

Nutrition for Track Cycling

Sprint track cycling involves a range of events from sprints to keirin to individual time trials. These events require intense efforts that generally last for less than 90 seconds
Longer track events such as scratch races and the Madison are better suited to endurance-trained cyclists and athletes competing in these events can follow the nutrition for road cycling.

Sprint track cycling relies on speed and strength and the ability to create a large power output. Power to weight ratio is important for sprint cyclists who aim to maximize muscle mass while keeping body fat levels reasonably low.

Sprint track cyclists will do most of their training on the track, in the gym and possibly on a stationary bike. Often training on the road is incorporated early in the season or to break up training to assist base fitness and maintain suitable body composition.

Training Diet

The aims of the training diet are to balance energy intake for high quality training and recovery, to enhance strength gains and training adaptations, and to maintain appropriate body fat levels. The training diet should be nutrient dense and provide a variety of foods from all food groups.

The training diet does not need to include the large amount of carbohydrate typical of road cyclists. Inadequate carbohydrate stores would rarely be a limiting factor to sprint performance. Sprint track cyclists should consume 3-4g carbohydrate/kg body weight/day, depending on training phase.

If longer duration training sessions are incorporated into training programs, carbohydrate requirements will increase.

Sprint track cyclists have relatively high protein requirements to gain and maintain muscle mass and strength. Lean red meat, chicken, fish and low fat dairy products provide good amounts of high quality protein.

To help achieve appropriate body fat levels, sprint track cyclists should limit energy dense foods including chocolate, pastries, soft drinks, alcohol and takeaways. These foods can add excess calories and contribute to higher than desirable body fat levels.

Fluid Needs
'Tracks' or velodromes can be indoors or outdoors, therefore conditions vary considerably. Fluid requirements vary considerably dependent on volume and type of training and the environment. Athletes need to know their individual fluid requirements to avoid under or over consuming fluids.

Fluid intake in the pits between races and during training is important but excessive fluid intake is not required and could leave a cyclist bloated or uncomfortable.

What Should you Eat Pre-Event?
Carbohydrate is rarely a limiting fuel source in a sprint event. For sprint events the pre-event meal should leave the athlete

comfortable and psychologically ready for the event more so than providing any particular mix or amount of macronutrients.

The pre-event meal should be eaten 2-3 hours prior to the warm up, and foods lower in fat and fiber are generally better tolerated. For example, fruit salad + yogurt, breakfast cereal with skim milk

What Should you Eat/Drink During Competition?
Often athletes will be racing several times over a day and there is plenty of opportunity to eat and drink between races.

If the competition is stretched over a whole or several days, the athlete needs to ensure adequate carbohydrate, protein and fluid are maintained over this time. The total amount of carbohydrate/protein required over the day would be consistent with training days. Racing schedules may interfere with regular meal times and smaller meals and snacks between races may be more appropriate.

If the time between races is short then drinking fluids such as a sports drink rather than eating is appropriate.

Nervous athletes or those unable to eat during a competition may benefit from sports food supplements such as bars or gels to maintain appropriate energy intake during competition. However, these are not usually necessary in addition to normal meals and snacks

Excess food and/or carbohydrate beverages during breaks and over the competition day could contribute to excess energy and consequently weight gain and/or leave the athlete bloated/uncomfortable

What About Recovery?
Recovery from a day of racing is important especially if racing again the next day. Recovery nutrition includes both between races and at the end of a day of racing.

Being prepared with appropriate food, fluid and supplement choices is a good strategy. Regular foods such as sandwiches, yogurt, cereal bars, and low fat milk drinks are useful. Some specialized sports foods containing protein and carbohydrates such as powerbar performance bar may also be appropriate especially if appetite is suppressed after high intensity racing. Being prepared can help prevent a trip to the food stall and potentially dangerous temptations! After a day of racing a substantial meal including both carbohydrate and protein such as with meat & vegetables or baked fish with salad and rice is also important to assist with recovery.

Other Nutrition Tips

Supplements are used widely in road and track cycling, with some being well researched and supported by science while others are poorly researched. It is important to be completely aware of the ingredients and legality of any supplements (including herbs, vitamins and minerals) taken.

Reference: Sports Dietitians

My Nutrient Requirements

- Based on 172 lbs body weight:
- Resting Caloric Expenditure (RCE) = 1, 892 calories
- Daily Activities Caloric Expenditure (DA) = 284 calories
- Workout Caloric Expenditure (WCE) = 598 calories
- Daily Caloric Expenditure (DCE) = 2,774 calories

The different nutrient timing phases are:

The Energy Phase - coincides with your workout. The primary metabolic objective of the muscle during this phase is to release sufficient energy to drive muscle contraction.

The Anabolic Phase - is the forty five minutes window post

117

exercise where your muscle machinery, with the right combination of nutrients, initiates the repair of damaged muscle protein and replenishes muscle glycogen stores.

The Growth Phase - extends from the end of the Anabolic Phase to the beginning of the next workout. It is the time when the muscle enzymes are involved in increasing the number of contractile proteins and the size of muscle fibers, as well as in helping the muscle fully replenish muscle glycogen depleted during the Energy Phase.

Chapter 10 – Aerodynamics

As a private pilot I had to learn the basics of aerodynamics – Bernoulli's principle being one of them where a liquid speeds up in a constricted zone to create areas of high pressure and low pressure, this same principle is what creates aerodynamic lift on an airplane's specially curved wing. Also I had to learn about barometric pressure, pressure altitude and density altitude and how they affect an airplanes performance. The same applies for humans riding a bicycle while generating power to provide acceleration to move through the same atmospheric conditions.

Barometric Pressure

Barometric pressure (also known as atmospheric pressure) is the force exerted by the atmosphere at a given point. It is known as the "weight of the air". A barometer measures barometric pressure. Measurement of barometric pressure can be expressed in millibars(mb) or in inches or millimeters of mercury (Hg). Normal pressure at sea level is 1013.3 millibars or 29.92 inches of mercury. Fluctuations in barometric pressure are usually a sign of weather conditions. A rise in pressure usually means improving weather while falling pressure may reflect impending inclement weather. Barometric pressures will also vary with altitude and moisture.

Air Density

Another major item we have to pay attention to is Air Density. Air Density affects aircraft performance. An aircraft uses up more runway to take off or land at altitude or on hot days at sea level where the air is less dense and where there is a decrease in aerodynamic resistance.

A combination of high altitude and high temperature could spell disaster for an uninformed pilot. The combination of high attitude and high temperature produces a situation that drastically reduces the aerodynamic performance of an airplane. But on the other hand this is a good thing for cyclists since cyclists will go faster under these conditions if they are acclimated to the conditions.

Air Density is the mass per unit volume of Earth's atmosphere. Atmospheric pressure (Barometric Pressure) is the amount of downward force exerted by the weight of the air above us and is measured in inches of mercury using a Barometer.

Air density decreases with an increase in altitude, it also decreases with increasing temperature or humidity. Warm air is less dense than cold air because there are fewer air molecules in a given volume of warm air than in the same volume of cooler air. Why am I mentioning Air Density? It is because Air Density is a factor in aerodynamic drag.

As you go up in elevation, the Air Density lessens and the resistance to movement is reduced. It therefore takes less energy to overcome drag at altitude than at sea level. However at altitude oxygen pressure becomes limited so aerobic performance will suffer unless you become acclimated. On the other hand in cycling events which are short and anaerobic such as 200m match sprint, kilometer and 500m time trials, the times at elevation will be faster than at sea level due to the reduction in Air Density.

Kissena track is an outdoor bumpy track at sea level, so one cannot expect super fast times there. Expect times to be considerably slower during opening weekend in late April when the temperatures are still cool and the air more dense than during the state championships in August when the temperatures are hot and the air less dense.

Fig 39: Carbon fiber bicycles at Kissena

One might think the times are slower on opening weekend because the racers haven't been training, but many of the racers who will be at Kissena Track opening day have already started racing road races starting the last week of February. So they are coming to opening weekend with a high level of fitness, but it will be the increased air density of the cool air which will result in slower times for the timed events.

In summary - a cyclist will perform better in hot weather and high altitudes in timed events since there is less aerodynamic drag if they are acclimated to the conditions. An aircraft will not perform well in hot weather and high altitudes since there are not enough air molecules and a decrease in aerodynamic resistance to help create lift within given operating parameters. The air resistance acting on a rider is directly related to the density of the air, the greater the density, the greater the force. Under standard conditions, the air's density at altitude is less than at sea level. Air density depends on temperature, barometric pressure and altitude and to some extent on water vapor (humidity). Air

121

re as a function of temperature,
and altitude, neglecting the effect of water
all.

son between the human body and a normally aspirated
engine such as that found in the Cessna 172 will find
the same air is used to produce energy and like humans these
normally aspirated airplane engines lose power as altitude
increases. As altitude increases the airplane engine runs out of
breath caused by the reduced air density, this is where turbo
charging an engine comes into play to maintain the same
conditions as found at sea level. Humans also need to turbo
charge or acclimatize their bodies to deal with the conditions at
altitude. They can train at altitude to increase red blood cells or
they can take drugs such as EPO that create more red blood cells
as many riders in the Tour de France do. You can use a $40
Oximeter to measure the oxygen level (or oxygen saturation) in
the blood by placing it on your fingertip. The normal range for
Oxygen saturation in the blood is 95 to 100%.

In the future I can see athletes being able to monitor the gases
they exhale in everyday training in order to see how fuel is being
burned in their bodies and what sort of energy sources are being
used to provide energy. This can then be adjusted accordingly by
varying intensity through an rpm charge or through a resistance
change. This is already being done in sports science institutes to
measure an athlete's exercise capacity through metabolic profile
testing and sweat analysis. This enables you to determine your
optimal fat and sustainable caloric burn zone (exercise heart rate)
to effectively manage your energy expenditure and electrolyte
and fluid replacement. Similar to how you can adjust the fuel to
air mixture in small aircraft to optimize flight endurance, speed
and fuel flow based on varying atmospheric conditions.

Fig 40: Riders training at Kissena

Chapter 11 – Velodrome Conditions

Velodrome Size and Surface Treatment:
In general there are no fixed standards for the length of a track. The track has to be individually designed in order to suit the demands of the respective project. The choice of the track length and its form will be influenced by the intended use, the category of track desired and economical aspects.

In practical terms the choice of a track length should be such, that the multiplication of half -or preferably- full laps, will result in a round figure of 1000 meters.

Shorter tracks are spectator-friendly. The racing is confined to a smaller area with the spectators being closer to the action. This generates a more intimate atmosphere between the racing cyclists and the spectators and produces more excitement. In addition smaller tracks and velodromes are naturally cheaper and easier to install.

Track Sizes:
- 125 meters
- 133.333 meters
- 142.857 meters
- 153.846 meters
- 166.666 meters
- 181.818 meters
- 200 meters
- 222.222 meters
- 250 meters
- 285.714 meters
- 333.333 meters
- 400 meters
- 500 meters

Velodrome Surfaces:

Wood, synthetics and concrete are all possible materials used to cover velodrome tracks. The newer the track, the more likely it is to be covered in wood or synthetics. The less expensive tracks employ concrete, asphalt, grass or, in some cases, cinder.

Fig 41: Kissena Velodrome

My Experience with Asphalt & Concrete:

The question is how does a bike handle on various velodrome surfaces with different banking and length. I have never ridden on a wooden velodrome so I guess there is a learning curve regarding wheels, tires and other equipment selection in dealing with wooden surfaces. For example the Mavic IO five bladed spoke wheel is primarily designed for riding on indoor velodromes which are more than likely to have a wooden surface. Also special tires, or special prepping of tires might be needed for wooden surfaces.

Riding on Kissena velodrome is like riding on the road since the surface is asphalt paving. Riding at Lehigh Velodrome is much smoother since the surface is concrete paving. It would seem logical that if you can ride a fast time at Kissena then you can ride an even faster time on a smoother track. Also different surfaces are affected differently by climatic conditions, which will affect how tires roll. Wood and synthetic surfaces would probably be the most stable surfaces in an indoor velodrome where temperature and humidity is controlled.

Fig 42: T-Town Velodrome

There is always a learning curve at any track which requires individual experimentation. What might work for someone else will not work for you. I rode a 12.57 using the inside line at Kissena and then rode a 12.85 at Lehigh Velodrome using the same inside line with the same equipment and same 108" gear - I was disoriented with the bike feel on the smooth concrete surface, bankings and the shorter track which reduced the length of back and home straights. I need to get more familiar with the Lehigh Velodrome before venturing onto a wooden velodrome.

Chapter 12 – Road Miles

You do have to maintain your aerobic base with rides of 2 hours or more. At the same time using whatever down hills come along to do some high speed cadence work in order to convert power to speed. This can also be simulated on the indoor spin bicycle.

Fig 43: Riders training at Kissena

I don't get anything for free nor do I get a discount for any cycling products. So whatever I recommend has to be good value for the money. I am just an ordinary recreational bike racer / track racer so it might be presumptuous of me to say I endorse products. But I have found Specialized products which I have used so far to be the best value for the money. Their road bikes of which I have the Tarmac and Roubaix, their shoes, their helmets, their pumps, and their sunglasses are all great products backed by good warranties which can only be provided by big reputable outfits like Specialized. Of course there might be better products which are more expensive, but when you have to spend scarce dollars on cycling products, you tend to look for value and return on investment. Also you have to wade through all the advertising hype, gimmicks and misinformation promoted by manufacturers and athletes who are later busted for drug use such as Lance Armstrong. After all the business of cycling is to sell the ordinary Joe Blow products at super inflated prices which are advertised in races like the Tour de France and Magazines.

For Track racing - a custom track bike can't be beat in terms of value for the money and fit. Mavic Ellipse clincher track wheels are also great value for the money. Wouldn't it be nice to own a set of top of the line Mavic IOs and disk, but where does one get $6,000 dollars to plop down on wheels?

Garmin - the Garmin Edge 305 GPS has helped to improve my track cycling, although it can become erratic at times over 30 mph due to the fast accelerations on the track. There is nothing like downloading the data from the Garmin - analyzing it and then using that information to modify your training. They have now entered the power meter market with pedals that measure power. Personally I feel all power measuring products are overpriced and not great value for the money. I am not going to pay $2000 for Power Tap, or $1600 dollars for Garmin Pedals when I can get a brand new bicycle for less money, it just doesn't make economic sense.

There are many books dedicated to training and racing on the road such as the ones by Joel Friel.

Chapter 13 – Race Day

The flying 200 meter time trial (so-called because riders have a flying start, as opposed to the standing start in the kilo and 500 meter) is rarely held on its own. The flying 200 meter is more commonly used as the qualifying event for the sprint competition, or as part of an Omnium competition. Velodromes have a line painted across the track at 200 meters before the finish line, for this purpose. How long the track is will determine where the 200-meter line is (for 250 meter tracks, it is about two-thirds of the way through the first bend; for 200 meter tracks, it is the finish line; for 400 meter tracks, it is the start line in the back straight). The clock will start as they cross this line, and finish when they reach the finish line.

Riders generally have two laps to build up speed before the clock starts. They will ride around the very top of the track as they near the start line, then drop down to the bottom in order to gain as much speed as possible from rolling down the steep inclined banking. The Flying 200 meter is ridden on a standard track bike (drop handlebars, spoked front wheel) when it is part of the Sprint competition, and often during the Omnium as well so riders need have only one bike.

A fast time at elite level is around 11 seconds for men, 12 seconds for women. At Olypmic and World level times have reached in the 9 second mark for men and 11 seconds for women.

The record for the fastest flying 200m time trial was set by <u>Kévin Sireau</u> (9.650) and <u>Grégory Baugé</u> (9.654) in <u>Moscow, Russia</u> on May 29th, 2009, beating the previous record of 9.772 set by <u>Theo Bos</u> at the same velodrome in 2006. Fast forward to Agua Caliente, Mexico 2014 – Francois Pervis rode a **9.3 seconds** flying 200m time trial and a **56.3 seconds** kilometer.

Fig 44: A scratch race at Kissena

Riding a flying 200 meter at Kissena Track
All your preparations are done and you have warmed up, the
sweat is pouring down your head. You are staged adjacent the
start and finish line, your heart is beating at over 160 BPM and
you haven't even started your effort. You nervously look at the
flags to note which way the wind is blowing and how strong.
You hope the wind would die down when it is your turn to circle
the track. Unfortunately the wind is messing with your head by
reversing direction and velocity.

The whistle is blown, it is your turn - you are now cruising
around on the banking of the track, trying to avoid swallowing
any bees which hang out by turn one, and then swiftly you focus
your attention to that overhanging tree branch at turn two which
could smack you off your bicycle. On the back stretch you check
that the coast is clear of any slithering snakes, yes snakes, there
have been a couple of small snakes doing a 100 meter dash along
the back stretch every now and then. Up comes turn three and
you scour the area for any slow moving baby turtles, they have

been known to cross your path. At turn four you are reminded that a sewer pipe is buried beneath as you gently roll over the bump. This bump requires some finesse to negotiate at high speed, hit it wrong and your bike will fish tail or worse.

Now you are approaching the start and finish line for the second time, you are going faster and you glance nervously over to the flags to check on the wind, not that it matters, you are already committed to your effort. You jump hard as you cross the start and finish line and you are now on your way at full speed at the bottom of the track, over the same path you just scoped out. Your time is yelled out as you finish - it is slooooow. Upon checking your gearing, you had forgotten to change your warm up gear to race gear.

Average speeds needed for various flying 200 meter times

- 9.5 seconds = 47.09 mph
- 9.6 seconds = 46.60 mph
- 9.7 seconds = 46.12 mph
- 9.8 seconds = 45.65 mph
- 9.9 seconds = 45.19 mph
- 10.0 seconds = 44.73 mph
- 10.1 seconds = 44.30 mph
- 10.2 seconds = 43.86 mph
- 10.3 seconds = 43.43 mph
- 10.4 seconds = 43.01 mph
- 10.5 seconds = 42.60 mph
- 10.6 seconds = 42.20 mph
- 10.7 seconds = 41.81 mph
- 10.8 seconds = 41.42 mph
- 10.9 seconds = 41.04 mph
- 11.0 seconds = 40.67 mph
- 11.1 seconds = 40.31 mph
- 11.2 seconds = 39.95 mph
- 11.3 seconds = 39.59 mph

- 11.4 seconds = 39.24 mph
- 11.5 seconds = 38.90 mph
- 11.6 seconds = 38.57 mph
- 11.7 seconds = 38.24 mph
- 11.8 seconds = 37.91 mph
- **11.9 seconds = 37.59 mph - my target time for 2014**
- 12.0 seconds = 37.28 mph
- 12.1 seconds = 36.97 mph
- 12.2 seconds = 36.67 mph
- 12.3 seconds = 36.37 mph
- 12.4 seconds = 36.07 mph
- **12.5 seconds = 35.79 mph - my 2009 season best time**
- 12.6 seconds = 35.51 mph
- 12.7 seconds = 35.22 mph
- 12.8 seconds = 34.95 mph
- 12.9 seconds = 34.68 mph
- 13.0 seconds = 34.41 mph
- 13.1 seconds = 34.15 mph
- 13.2 seconds = 33.89 mph
- 13.3 seconds = 33.64 mph
- 13.4 seconds = 33.38 mph
- **13.5 seconds = 33.13 mph - my 2008 season best time**
- 13.6 seconds = 32.89 mph
- 13.7 seconds = 32.66 mph
- 13.8 seconds = 32.42 mph
- 13.9 seconds = 32.18 mph
- 14.0 seconds = 31.95 mph

Sprinting

Track racing is essentially for sprinters, short match sprint events or scratch races which require bursts of sustained speed. At least these are the spectator friendly events. Events such as the Pursuit and other Time Trial events are more for the athletes rather than spectators, these timed events can be quite boring to watch.
Track racers are into speed, direct drive speed, fast twitch speed, in your face speed.

Some of us spend time in the gym trying to build strength and muscles for sprinting. Undoubtedly, strong muscles mean power, power means speed which results in a good jump and acceleration on the track. That is the good part - on the flip side an abundant of strength and power can lead to clumsiness and impulsiveness if not combined with flexibility, leg speed, agility and temperament. One has to be patient and employ the right tactics at the right time to gain the edge. Also you have to be confident, believe in your training and don't second guess yourself.

Your jump might be excellent, but your tactics, and bike handling skills can be a problem. In three up sprints you might want to jump too early or just use the wrong tactics altogether. In three up sprints there are more variables involved and you have to be able to cover all bases. Two up sprints require different tactics, if poor tactics are used by the stronger, faster rider then that rider does not necessarily win. A scratch race on the other hand is all about conserving ATP (Adenosine Triphosphate), the chemical compound which provides energy to your muscle fibers which allows for maximum contraction in the last 10 to 20 seconds of the sprint. Sometimes you make your move too early, burn up all your ATP while others sitting in your draft come around you.

This is where an external pair of eyes in the form of a good coach comes in handy. A coach who is present at the track to observe what you are doing wrong or right and to help you correct your mistakes. Many of us cannot afford to have a coach at our disposal. So instead we pick up bits and pieces here and there. Or use a video camera to analyze the ride, it is always a learning experience looking at a video of your race from a different perspective.

Registration:
Training during the year to prepare for the racing season can all be ruined by forgetting to do some important pre-race day and

race day preparations. I usually use a check list to get my short term preparations in order. To race at Kissena Track one has to pre-register online at Bikereg.com. This step can be easily forgotten and you could be out of luck come race day. I usually place a reminder in my phone the day before and of course keep an eye on the weather for rain, no racing takes place in the rain. Online registration is also required for the weekly Wednesday evening races, you can register for the whole season or you can register for individual Wednesdays. Keep in mind there are always about four Wednesdays per year, which are rained out due to cyclical weather patterns. Also it would be unwise to register for the whole season if you have a work or school schedule which does not guarantee you time to race every Wednesday evening.

Get Bicycle Ready:
I usually go through a routine the day before where I get the bicycle ready. I make sure my warm up gear is on, tires are pumped up, all nuts and bolts are tightened. Bumpy Kissena track has a tendency of loosening your nuts and also bruising them – pun intended. So make sure you use chamois cream on the tender parts and also make sure your chain is clean and lubed. In the case of a Keirin type chain which does not have a master link, but instead a nut and bolt – make sure this nut and bolt is tight. When the chain is new the nut and bolt has a tendency to loosen. Make sure your wheels are on tightly but be careful to not over torque when tightening wheels to frame, you can easily shear the spindle. Finally make sure the bicycle is clean and free of dirt, you don't want any extraneous material which will create even a little bit of drag. Also walk with an extra set of wheels, should you get a flat. Apart from a crash, a flat can ruin your day at the races.

Organize Bag:
Once bicycle is ready, you now have to get the supporting cast in order. I have a bag with multiple pockets to organize my cast of characters such as tools, pump, helmet, duct tape, tie wraps, stop watch, gloves, shoe covers, Garmin Edge 305 GPS, cameras,

phone, helmet cover, shoes, shoe cover, paper towels, rags. Also within this bag I have a chain ring pouch which holds my various chain rings, cogs, spare chain, chain link remover, lock rings, gear chart and note book to write down key training notes, gearing and racing activities / results. The Garmin Edge 305 GPS records the rest of racing parameters for later analysis. The chain rings I carry – 53, 52, 51, 50, 49, 48 & 47. The cogs I carry – 16, 15, 14, 13 & 12. Using some of these gear combinations might require you to change your chain length, I try to avoid this by choosing gear ratios which use one chain length. Not to forget my racing license is tucked away in the gear bag since the bag always follows me to the races - no license no racing.

Trainers or Rollers:
You do have to take a turbo trainer or rollers with you, since track racing is all about waiting around for your event. You need to keep your legs race ready and the blood flowing in between events, this can only be achieved with trainers or rollers since the track will be occupied with other races. A warm up allows for a period of adjustment, gradually increasing heart rate, boosting muscle temperature, improving blood flow, redistributing blood to active muscles, and enhancing the delivery of nutrients to cells. It should last at least five to 10 minutes to prepare the body for what's to come. It also provides a psychological cue, preparing the brain for higher intensity levels. Consequently, a warm up enhances performance. A warm up should be sport specific, meaning that the gestures involved mimic the activity you're about to do.

A cool-down prevents post-exercise venous blood pooling and an excessively fast drop in blood pressure, which combined helps reduce the chance of light-headedness or fainting. Plus it helps bring down the heart rate slowly, minimizing the chance of muscle spasms or cramping. A cool-down should last at least five minutes. Cooling down is similar to warming up in that you can do the same movements outlined in the warm up above but at a slower pace and lower intensity.

Keeping Cool:

A chair with a sun cover is my item of choice for protection from the sun. It can get really hot at the track with heat rising from the asphalt and sucking the moisture out of your body. If the temperature is an ambient 90 degrees, then expect the heat off the asphalt to be about 115 degrees. Sitting in the grass can help to mitigate some of the reflected heat, also the better option is to sit on the grassy area under a portable tent. Nothing affects performance negatively more than heat and dehydration which also drives my pulse rate way up in to the nether zones. A Cooler is brought along with multiple bottles of cold water, Gatorade, ice packs, gels and snack bars. No Beer, Red Bull or caffeinated energy drinks, this is a one way ticket to dehydration. A typical Sunday track meet will last about five hours, so the snack bars and gels will have to provide energy, because I don't seem to have an appetite for anything more substantial, maybe because the blood is not available for digesting real food.

Pre-Race:

I always plan to arrive one hour before start of event, this will give me ample time to sign in, set up shop in my favorite spot, hopefully a shaded one. Once set up, get into my racing attire, assemble bicycle, check tire pressures and head onto the track after looking right for traffic which might t-bone me. In the warm up gear I do a 20 lap warm up progressively increasing speed to a final lap sprint, or jump into a pace line, this takes about 15 minutes. Next comes three to four jumps of increasing distance – 100 meters, 200 meters, 300 meters and 400 meters. Now it is time to head off the track and change gear to race gear and get a drink. Once in race gear I do another five laps of easy rolling and a couple of tempered jumps just to get the muscle memory going. This is my typical warm up for mass start events, but I would adjust these if the events are the flying 200 meter or the kilo. If I timed my warm up correctly I would hear the bell ring for the start of the events. This is when I will place my bike on the trainer or rollers and continue to spin if I am not racing. All the while making sure I am drinking lots of fluids to stay hydrated, because at Kissena on a hot day the sweat pours off of you like an open tap. Electrolyte tablets might also be a good choice under these conditions, to prevent cramps.

Fig 45: A Women's Scratch race at Kissena

Race:
I am all exited if it is a scratch race and dejected if it is a miss & out or some other endurance type race such as points, snow ball, snow flake, devil catch me and burn me...blah blah blah. At least I know I have a chance of winning or placing in a scratch race, but forget it with the endurance type events which require good short term recovery. My focus this year is the flying 200 meter, the match sprints and the Kilo. Unfortunately you don't score upgrade points in these events. Upgrade points are only scored in mass start categorized events where there are ten or more riders. Mass start masters events do not score upgrade points.

Post Event:
Put your warm down gear on the bicycle and warm down before retracing your steps and heading home. Also your warm down gear, which is your warm up gear will be on the bicycle for the

next training session or race meet.

Cameras:
I always walk with a camera to the races to record some of the action, be it a little point and shoot camera, SLR camera or video camera. Sometimes I give the camera to a spectator and ask them to just snap away. As you get older you tend to want to record challenging activities which you take part in, since you know you would not be able to continue doing as the years go by and bones start to creak. It is always good to look back in time and marvel at the fact that you once did that. In the age of digital photography it is easy to take and share images.

Retrospective:
Ironically, all that I wrote above, I did none of it back in the 80s when I was in my 20s. I rode to the track in my race gear, my race wheels strapped to my back with an old tubular. Can't remember where I got water from, managed to still race with good results and ride back home.

The Kilometer Time Trial - Some Basics:
Larger chain rings are harder to accelerate, especially from standing starts. You will not be able to accelerate as fast with a large chain ring as with a smaller.

Large chain ring = slower pick up while small chain ring = faster pick up.

Pursuiters and endurance riders tend to ride bigger gears / chain rings due to the fact that acceleration is not the key factor in their events, all they have to do is get on top of the gear and roll along. There was one master who rode the kilo this past weekend in a 56 x 15, he is a specialist pursuiter - I believe the 56 chain ring is a road chain ring – how much bigger can they get?

A 94" gear can be achieved in two combinations – (45x13 = 93.5") or (49x14=94.5"). Obviously the 45 x 13 would be easier to accelerate as in a match sprint while the 49x14 would be harder to accelerate but easier to roll once it gets going as in a time trial. So that leaves the question – what is the right gear to use? It all depends on the time of year, weather conditions, level of fitness and your leg speed / optimal cadence range.

So once the gear selection is made, the next thing to focus on is your getaway speed. Standing start work is required and transitioning from standing to seated. This phase is highly unstable since you are moving at a fastest rate of speed for the kilo event. Transitioning from standing to seated and then into the aero bars at over 30 mph takes practice; the bumpiness of the track doesn't help. You also want to get on top of the gear and reach your maximum speed before you sit down.

Don't worry too much about fading at the end, everyone fades after 700 to 750 meters in the kilo so it's just about hanging on for the last 200 to 250 meters and concentrating on technique during this phase which is known as the dead phase or stop the car and let me out phase. Endurance training will help with this. Also it is a good idea during the winter and during the season to do flying laps in the aero bars – build speed at the top of the track, accelerate down the bank and sit down on the start / finish line at 30 mph, maintain this speed for the lap, concentrating on sticking to the white line.

Of course sticking to the white line is easier said than done. In the banking you will tend to drift up track, you will want to control this drift to no more than halfway between the white and red line. The white line is the shortest path around the track, sponges are placed at the bottom of the track in the turns to prevent you from cheating, as in riding on the inside blue band. At Kissena it is hard to hold a tight line in aero bars because of the bumps, I end up riding closer to the red line to prevent going wide. I might even consider going back to regular track bars just to maintain control and to ride closer to the white line since that is the shortest path around the track. Even my flying 200 meter I ride the red line to carry speed and maintain control since the track is also very shallow - 19 degrees banking at the steepest part.

Warm up for the Kilometer Time Trial

- Warming up on the Turbo Trainer/Rollers is the norm for Track Cycling, however it is optimum you try and take the Road Bike to the event as well for warm-up/cool-down.

- One hour before first event – 20 laps or 30 minutes easy gear on road bike or 80-85 inch gear on track bike, end with 5 Second high cadence sprint. Take five minutes rest - drink fluids.

- Track Effort – Flying 100 meter efforts on your track bike using the same gear. If you cannot get to the track, then do 2 minutes on trainer / rollers followed by a 10 second sprint interval. Follow up with 2 minutes recovery.

- Change gear to race gear and wheels, eat and drink something.

- Track Effort – Rolling standing start from pursuit line to start line (first four pedal strokes), again if you can't get to the track then repeat the above 2 minutes on trainer/ rollers followed by a 10 second sprint interval to get the lactic acid flowing. Follow up with 2 minutes easy session in race gear / wheels on trainer / rollers. The whole point of doing this is to get your body primed and used to buffering the lactic acid this way you can go all out from the start of your event without suffering the consequences of not priming the body for the exertion. After all the kilo is an all out 100% effort from start to finish with no time for rest.

- Take 10 minutes rest, relax, and sit with feet up, headphones on to get in the zone.

- Then do 10 minutes very easy on trainer / rollers or road bike, remembering to drink, this should leave you with 5 minutes to go, all you need to do is put your helmet on, and wait for officials to call you.

On Deck

Waiting on deck can be stressful since you timed your warm up completion in time for your kilo. Keep your fingers crossed that you don't get sent to the back straight to start your kilo. This entails hiking across the Kissena glades with bike, hopefully keeping your cleats from getting clogged with dirt, of course the hike causes your heart rate to rise and you haven't even started your event. Try to relax and get your heart rate down while waiting for your start, if possible sit, usually some deep breathing exercises will help with this. All the while you are going through a mental checklist of things you need to do. I tend to get tunnel vision when it is my turn to start, so much so that I sometimes forget to start my Garmin before the effort. In any case instinct takes over from all the practice sessions.

Start – 200 meter

On deck for the start - already I am having trouble clipping into my pedals and cinching the supplemental toe straps. Don't want to snap out of my pedals, these are top of the line Shimano Dura Ace babies, unlike the cheap Nashbar LOOK compatible look a likes which caused me to lose a match sprint two years ago when my right foot came flying out – shudder - that could have ended bad. I always start with my left leg in the front, although my right leg is stronger. The reason for this - the force from the left leg causes the bike to drift in rather than outwards.

The official yells - Rider Ready – Flag Up – Gun Up – POW! (We definitely need to get a five second count down at Kissena, possibly an iPod hooked up to a loud speaker would do the trick) I'm off, head up staring straight ahead, making some combat

141

breathing grunts and funny faces, elbows and arms straight as if doing a set of dead lifts as I apply downward force with one leg while pulling back and up with the other; the front wheel starts to wobble as the speed picks up. By turn two I am over 30 mph and I sit, although I could have stood a little longer to get on top of the gear. I gingerly get into the aero position as the first 200 meter segment approaches – count ONE! (Four segments to go)

200 - 400 meter
I am flying like a jet, the rear disk is singing as I navigate the turn on approach to the 400 meter marker. I flash by the 400 meter segment – someone yelled go Mike – count TWO! (Three segments to go)

400 - 600 meter
I am starting to slow as if told by air traffic control to slow for approach to landing. The 600 meter segment is approaching, but not as quickly as I would like. Who put lead in my rear wheel? – count THREE! (Two segments to go)

600 - 800 meter
I am finding it very difficult to ride a straight line. The front wheel has a mind of its own; the wind isn't helping much in this department either. The 800 meter segment approaches as I start to see spots, trying to get oxygen into my body – count FOUR! (One segment to go)

800 - 1000 meter
By now it felt like I've touched down, and the drag chutes are deployed, where is that damn finish line? My legs feel like they are going around in slow motion – wait they are going around in slow motion as the 1000 meter red pursuit finish line approaches – count FIVE! (Its over) – oops I can't forget to press the stop button on the Garmin- I hope I have some good data to analyze. As you noticed I mentally count the segments to give me an idea of when the torture will be over. Kissena is a 400 meter track, so if you start on one end you will end up finishing on the opposite end. I have seen a few people get confused and finished short of

where they were supposed to finish – they did 2 laps instead of 2 ½ laps.

Fig 46: Rider finishing the flying 200m event at Kissena

Warm down
I ride around the track for a lap at the top of the bank to get systems back to normal levels, get off the track, place bike on trainer and spin easy to flush the legs, all the while pondering if I would be able to do the next race or just call it a day -the Killermeter just killed my legs.

Analysis of a Kilometer Time Trial

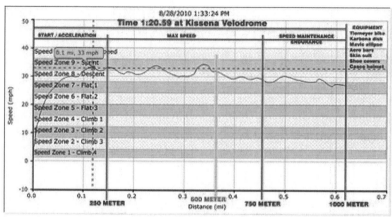

Fig 47: Analysis of a Kilometer time trial at Kissena

From profile above - I would need to get a better start to accelerate up to a higher speed (to about 35 mph) by 250 meters. This is easily achievable since the strength and gym work I do would come into play, but then I would pay for this effort towards the end of the kilo. I tend to be conservative with my starts because I want to minimize how much I fade towards the end. At my current level of fitness, I know if I go out too hard, then I am going to fade very badly since I don't have the endurance base required. I usually get up to my target speed and sit way too early. Profile shows I got up to a speed of 33 mph at about the 200 meter mark and then maintained that to about the 600 meter mark, where I then faded for the remaining 400 meters. I would need to work on my endurance to be able to finish strong in the last 400 meters. Also I would need to ride a tighter line closer to or on the white line which is the shortest path around the track. It is very difficult to do this using aero bars at Kissena, I always end up riding closer to the red line to maintain control. Riding on the rollers during the winter in the aero bars should help to develop the balance and finesse needed to ride a tighter line on the track. Also strong core muscles come into play during the last 400 meters where you have to maintain balance and still generate power from tired legs to propel the bike forward in an aero position.

Kilo training is a lot more complicated than it seems, the most important thing for a kilo rider is endurance, base training miles are needed consisting of 2 to 3 hour rides for about two months. The next phase would be sprinter specific gym training consisting of squats and other leg exercises. On the track you will have to do over geared short sprint efforts like 100 meter flying starts. By over geared workouts meaning no more that 4 inches above race gear, for example a race gear of 94 inches means 98 inches for over geared training. These efforts can be repeated on the road with big gear hill intervals. The next phase is speed, which consists of the same gym workouts but less weights and more reps and track workouts using a gear 4 inches less than race gear which would be 90 inches. It is important to remember that even though the rider's aerobic capacity is very important the kilo is still an anaerobic effort. So once you get to roughly 750 meters then the remaining distance is just about hanging on and maintaining technique in this dead phase. So training sessions that simulate the 'dead phase' are important, these can be achieved through motor pacing and flying efforts of increased distances.

Components of a Kilo:
- Start (initial power)
- Acceleration (to 250 meters)
- Max speed (250 to 750 meters)
- Speed maintenance / endurance (750 to 1000 meters)

In order to improve my Kilo, these are the components I would have to work on:

Start:
- Starts of varying distance (rolling and standing)
- Strength work in the gym and on bike (squats and over geared efforts on the bike)

- Power work in the gym (power cleans, plyometrics such as bounding up stairs or box jumps with and without weighted vest)

Acceleration:
- Repeated intervals from a slow roll up to a point where max speed is attained - basically 250 meters roll ups to about 35 mph in aero bars.
- Intervals which target VO2 max

Max speed:
- Flying start intervals of 800 meters at about 30 mph avg speed in aero bars

Speed maintenance:
- Flying start intervals of 1000 meters at about 30 mph avg speed in aero bars
- One long training ride of 2 to 3 hours per week to build endurance, leg speed & recovery
- Intervals of shorter distances with incomplete recovery (tabata intervals)

Simulation efforts on spin bike and in the gym:
- Simulate kilo efforts on the spin bike to measure power output.
- Simulate kilo efforts in gym using leg press machine while reducing the weight from heavy to medium to mimic a kilo effort on the bike for a duration of 1 minute 20 seconds. This should get the blood and lactic acid rushing to the head.

The 500 meter:
The 500M is pretty easy, just go hard and once again watch out for the red line white line thing. It is amazing how much harder it is to hold you line when going as fast as you do during these sprint time trials. An important thing to note during the standing start is to stand on the pedals with your arms and wrists locked in

a straight line and head up as if doing a dead lift with weights. This way you can transmit maximal initial force to the pedals to get the bike moving forward without wobbling. It is important to keep your wrists straight, if they are bent you will lose force transmission and hence power.

Mental imagery and music can help to keep you in the zone and focused for competition. This is a whole subject matter in itself that can be found in books dedicated to the subject of training your mind to make your body perform under stressful situations. It is also important to have fun and not make cycling a job. After all you are not getting paid as an Amateur even if you become State Champion, National Champion or World Champion. It is best to approach cycling for its health benefits rather than for its monetary rewards. Also you should spend some time to analyze the risks versus rewards.

Risk Analysis:
In flying we have to go through a logical set of pre-flight items to mitigate the risks before taking to the skies. The same strategy can be applied to cycling since there is a certain level of risk involved in training and racing. We use the **PAVE** checklist to analyze the risks of flying as part of the pre-flight.

PAVE is an evaluation checklist where the P = Pilot, A = Aircraft, V = Environment and E = External Pressures:

Pilot experience, recency and physical condition:
- How many takeoffs / landings done recently?
- Number of hours in make and model of aircraft?
- Instrument approaches and hours done recently?
- Terrain and airspace familiarity?
- Recent illness?
- Medication or drugs being used?
- Recent stressful events?
- Hours of sleep in last 24 hours?
- Alcohol use in last 24 hours?

- Recent food and water consumption?

Aircraft:
- How much fuel reserves do you have?
- Experience in type of aircraft?
- Familiarity with aircraft performance?
- Familiarity with aircraft equipment?
- Familiarity with aircraft avionics and GPS?
- Familiarity with aircraft autopilot?
- Familiarity with aircraft communication systems?
- Have the current charts for the flight?
- Have proper clothing for the flight?
- Have proper survival gear suitable for the flight?
- Have the required documents for the flight?
- Have the required inspections for the flight?
- Have the required equipment for the flight?

Environment:
- Airport conditions?
- Weather conditions?

External Pressures:
- Make adequate allowances for delays?
- Make adequate allowances for diversions or cancellations?
- Have the proper personal equipment?

With this information from the PAVE checklist you can now apply the 3P decision making model to analyze the risks and change them in your favor.

1. **Perceive** the hazards.
2. **Process** to evaluate level of risk.
3. **Perform** risk management to change the outcome in your favor.

This same strategy can be applied to your training and racing on the track. Let us alter the checklist for track cycling and call it the REVE checklist.

Rider experience, recency and physical condition:
- How many training sessions do you have on the track?
- Number of races you have taken part in on the track?
- Are you familiar with the track?
- Are you acclimated to the conditions?
- Recent illness?
- Medication or drugs being used?
- Recent stressful events?
- Hours of sleep in last 24 hours?
- Alcohol use in last 24 hours?
- Recent food and water consumption?

Equipment
- Familiarity with your bicycle performance and gears?
- Familiarity with your equipment?
- Familiarity with your bike computer / power meter?
- Have proper clothing for the ride / race?
- Have the required documents for the ride / race?
- Have the proper equipment for the ride / race?

Environment:
- Track conditions?
- Experience level of riders you are riding / racing with?
- Types of events you are riding?
- Weather conditions?

External Pressures:
- Make adequate allowances for delays?
- Make adequate allowances for race format changes?
- Food and water availability?

With this information from the REVE checklist you can now apply the 3P decision making model to analyze the risks and change them in your favor before the race and during the race.

1. Perceive the hazards. *(Example - too many inexperienced riders in the mass start events and you are not familiar with the track or the riders)*
2. Process to evaluate level of risk. *(Example – what races should I ride where I stand a chance of placing and not crashing?)*
3. Perform risk management to change the outcome in your favor. *(Example – ride only the masters events and time trials, stay away from the categorized events or stay at the front of the pack and follow a rider you are familiar with.)*

Conclusion:
Stay safe, healthy and have fun.

Fig 48: 1984 rider doing a kilo at Kissena – photo provided by Debbie & Larry DeSario

About the author

Michael Mahesh is a Masters Road and Track racing cyclist who started racing bicycles in 1986 in New York at the Kissena Velodrome. He has a Private Pilot license and a Bachelors Degree in Construction Management. He also played Soccer for his high school team, semi-professional cricket in Guyana and New York and has a brown belt in Karate.

Fig 49: 2004 Rider getting ready for a match sprint at Kissena

Fig 50: 2013 - A vintage looking track bicycle reminiscing at Kissena

References and Reading List

P9OX – Extreme Home Fitness program to help you lose weight and get strong in a short period of time. All you need is a set of dumbbells, a pull up bar, resistance bands and you are all set. The workout program comes with 12 DVDs which you can customize to your personal goals. The plyometrics and core synergistics are tough DVD workouts which are perfect for stimulating the cycling muscles used for explosive standing starts and sprints. I would highly recommend this program since it is like having a personal trainer in your living room and it encompasses every single thing included in the books below in a cohesive motivational program.

The Time Crunched Cyclist by Chris Carmichael – Get fit in less time, help build competitive fitness in six hours a week. You don't need endless miles on the road. You don't need endless hours in the gym. Who has the time with a full work schedule and family commitments?

The Ultimate Ride by Chris Carmichael – Helps build a strong foundation for incremental leaps in fitness, times, and techniques. Nutritional advice, goal setting methods, mental exercises and physical training tips.

Chris Carmichael training Videos – videos can either be bought and downloaded from the website or purchased on DVDs. These are great cycling workout videos targeting different energy systems using various types of intervals. These videos help to break up the monotony of riding the spin bike by simulating having a personal trainer.

The Mental Edge by Kenneth Baum – Maximizing your sports potential with the mind body connection. Your mind is your most valuable piece of equipment, your strongest muscle and your best shot at peak performance for life.

Nutrient Timing by John Ivy & Robert Portman – by timing specific nutrition to your muscle's 24 hour growth cycle. Deliver the precise amounts of nutrients needed at precisely the right time to optimize your muscle building agents and maximize muscle growth, while minimizing muscle damage and soreness after a hard workout.

High-Tech Cycling by Edmund R. Burke – a unique compilation of current information on the rapidly evolving sport of cycling. With topics ranging from equipment selection to the nuances of cycling bio mechanics.

The Cyclist's Training Bible 3rd Edition by Joel Friel – shows you how the benefits of a scientific, self coached training plan will refine your skills and improve your cycling performance.

Weight Training for Dummies by Liz Neporent – book on how to lift weights.

The New Power Program by Dr Michael Colgan – another weight lifting book which focuses on body posture and core strength.

Training and Racing with a Power Meter – Hunter Allen & Andrew Coggan – how to train with a power meter and interpret the data.

Racing Tactics for Cyclists by Thomas Prehn – helps cyclists avoid common race mistakes and ride intelligently.

Serious Cycling 2nd by Edmund R. Burke – go faster and train more efficiently by applying advanced science to your cycling. Take the latest scientific data in the sport and translate it into beneficial applications.

Heroes, Villains & Velodromes by Richard Moore – documentary style book about Chris Hoy and Britain's track cycling revolution. Also points out the high level of secrecy found in Track Cycling. This is more of a book about Chris Hoy's life story rather than training tips for Track Cycling, but still a very useful book.

USCF Introduction to Coaching Cyclists – this manual is the only book where there were about three pages dedicated to useful information pertaining to track cycling.

Functional Training for Sports by Michael Boyle – this book gives you training programs to reach a higher level of athleticism with functional training exercises. Boyle guides you through a complete system that focuses on training your body the way it will be used during competition to develop movement skills, body positions, and explosive power essential for all sports.

Core Performance by Mark Verstegen and Pete Williams – this book shows you how to develop balanced fitness, strength, muscle mass, flexibility, power and endurance without overemphasizing or shortchanging any component.

Useful Apps for smartphones:
- P90X
- Dartfish Express
- Bike Gears
- Endomondo
- RunKeeper
- Tabata Timer
- Weather Bug
- Strava
- Bike Repair

Fig 51: Masters National and World Champion – Kimberly Edwards training at Kissena, her home track and riding the "Affinity Kissena" track frame.

Glossary

Acceleration - The rate of change of the velocity of a moving body. An increase in the magnitude of the velocity of a moving body (an increase in speed) is called a positive acceleration; a decrease in speed is called a negative acceleration. Acceleration, like velocity, is a vector quantity, so any change in the direction of a moving body is also an acceleration. A moving body that follows a curved path, even when its speed remains constant, is undergoing acceleration.

ADP - in biological terms, is the abbreviation for the molecule known as adenosine diphosphate. When it gains another phosphate group, it creates ATP, which is used for energy.

Adrenaline - a hormone secreted by the adrenal glands, esp. in conditions of stress, increasing rates of blood circulation, breathing, and carbohydrate metabolism and preparing muscles for exertion.

Aerobic - The word aerobic literally means "with oxygen" or "in the presence of oxygen." Aerobic exercise is any activity that uses large muscle groups, can be maintained continuously for a long period of time and is rhythmic in nature. Aerobic activity trains the heart, lungs and cardiovascular system to process and deliver oxygen more quickly and efficiently to every part of the body. As the heart muscle becomes stronger and more efficient, a larger amount of blood can be pumped with each stroke. Fewer strokes are then required to rapidly transport oxygen to all parts of the body. An aerobically fit individual can work longer, more vigorously and achieve a quicker recovery at the end of the aerobic session.

Alactic Metabolism - Your cells store energy in the form of a compound called adenosine triphosphate, or ATP. Muscle cells store only enough ATP to fuel a few seconds of maximal work. However, they also store another compound called creatine phosphate, which rapidly replenishes ATP. Together, ATP and creatine phosphate comprise the alactic anaerobic energy system. The alactic system can supply energy for up to 10 seconds of muscle contraction. Once ATP and creatine phosphate stores are depleted, they must be replenished, either aerobically or through the lactate system.

Anaerobic - Oxygen is not present with anaerobic exercise. When we exercise anaerobically glycogen is used as fuel.

ATP - Adenosine Triphosphate (ATP) is the energy of life. It is a molecule that stores all the energy that comes from foods. It is present in every cell. It is estimated that more than 160 kg of ATP is formed in the body everyday.

Atrophy – is when muscles waste away. The main reason for muscle wasting is a lack of physical activity. This can happen when a disease or injury makes it difficult or impossible for you to move an arm or leg.

Cadence – he work required to move a bike down the road is measured in watts. To define it very simply, Watts = Force x Cadence, or how hard you press on the pedals multiplied by the number of times per minute (Revolutions Per Minute – RPM) you apply this force.

Cardiovascular - Cardiovascular is related to heart functioning and various blood vessels. It relates to the heart and the various blood vessels, like arteries and veins.

Dopamine – Dopamine is a neurotransmitter, one of those chemicals that is responsible for transmitting signals in between the nerve cells (neurons) of the brain.

Endorphins - any of a group of hormones secreted within the brain and nervous system and having a number of physiological functions. They are peptides that activate the body's opiate receptors, causing an analgesic effect.

Endurance - means the ability to sustain or withstand prolonged exercise for minutes to hours. There are different types of endurance, which include; aerobic endurance, anaerobic endurance, speed endurance and strength endurance. A sound basis of aerobic endurance is important for all events. Endurance helps to make the heart stronger and keeps blood pressure under control .This is by enabling the arteries to retain their elasticity, allowing for greater blood flow through them.

Flexibility - The ability of a joint to move through its full range of motion is defined as flexibility. Because each joint has a different potential range of motion, it is joint specific. Sometimes, being flexible in a particular area of the body requires the interaction of a series of joints. The range of motion in the back that yoga practitioners strive to achieve, for example, requires the development of flexibility along the entire spine.

Force - is a push or pull upon an object resulting from the object's interaction with another object. Whenever there is an interaction between two objects, there is a force upon each of the objects. When the interaction ceases, the two objects no longer experience the force. Forces only exist as a result of an interaction.

FTP - Functional threshold power is a key metric for cycling performance. Defined as the maximum average power a cyclist can maintain over a one-hour effort, functional threshold power is particularly important for time trial specialists and for short-course and Olympic distance triathletes who need to know how to pace their effort over thirty-to-sixty minutes.

Hypertrophy - involves an increase in size of skeletal muscle through an increase in the size of its component cells. Hypertrophy can be broken down into two types of categories: myofibrillar and sarcoplasmic. Each of these specific types of muscle hypertrophy will result in increasing size of cells, but not of equal effect. Sarcoplasmic hypertrophy is focused on

160

increasing the actual size of the muscle, and less on increasing strength. Myofibril hypertrophy will focus more on strength increase and less on an increase in the size of the skeletal muscle.

Hypoxia - The term hypoxia is a condition where the tissues are not oxygenated adequately, usually due to an insufficient concentration of oxygen in the blood. The oxygen deprivation can have severe adverse effects on various body cells that need to perform important biological processes.

Intervals - Interval training is a type of discontinuous physical training that involves a series of low- to high-intensity exercise workouts interspersed with rest or relief periods. The high-intensity periods are typically at or close to anaerobic exercise, while the recovery periods involve activity of lower intensity. Interval training can be described as short periods of work followed by rest. The main aim is to improve speed and cardiovascular fitness.

Lactate Metabolism – Muscle cells metabolize carbohydrates for energy by a process called glycolysis. The end product of glycolysis is a compound called pyruvate. Glycolysis is fast but inefficient, producing just two molecules of ATP from a single molecule of glucose, or blood sugar. When muscle cells have sufficient oxygen, they can break down pyruvate aerobically to yield many more ATP molecules. However, when oxygen isn't available, your cells convert pyruvate into lactic acid, which can accumulate in the form of lactate. Although lactate does not directly cause fatigue, when lactate builds up to high levels in your tissues during intense exercise, exhaustion quickly follows.

Lactate Threshold - or anaerobic threshold (AT)) is the exercise intensity at which lactate (more specifically, lactic acid) starts to accumulate in the blood stream. The reason for the acidification of the blood at high exercise intensities is two-fold: the high rates of ATP hydrolysis in the muscle release hydrogen ions, as they are co-transported out of the muscle into the blood via the MCT— monocarboxylate transporter, and also bicarbonate stores in the blood begin to be used up. This happens when lactate is produced faster than it can be removed (metabolized) in the muscle. When exercising at or below the LT, any lactate produced by the muscles is removed by the body without it building up.

Lactic Acid - Most of it is made by muscle tissue and red blood cells. When the oxygen level in the body is normal, carbohydrate breaks down into water and carbon dioxide. When the oxygen level is low, carbohydrate breaks down for energy and makes lactic acid.

Metabolic Rate - the amount of energy expended in a give period

Myofascia - Fascia or myofascia is the dense, tough tissue which surrounds and covers all of your muscles and bones. This outer fascial covering is very strong and very flexible. In fact, it has a tensile strength of over 2000 pounds.

Neuromuscular - relating to nerves and muscles.

Oximeter - an instrument for measuring the proportion of oxygenated hemoglobin in the blood

Periodization - is a method of alternating training loads to produce peak performance for a specific competitive event.

Plyometrics - also known as "jump training" or "plyos", are exercises based around having muscles exert maximum force in as short a time as possible, with the goal of increasing both speed and power

Power - the quantity work has to do with a force causing a displacement. Work has nothing to do with the amount of time that this force acts to cause the displacement. Sometimes, the work is done very quickly and other times the work is done rather slowly. For example, a rock climber takes an abnormally long time to elevate her body up a few meters along the side of a cliff. On the other hand, a trail hiker (who selects the easier path up the mountain) might elevate her body a few meters in a short amount of time. The two people might do the same amount of work, yet the hiker does the work in considerably less time than the rock climber. The quantity that has to do with the rate at which a certain amount of work is done is known as the power. The hiker has a greater power rating than the rock climber.

Program - a planned series of projects, future events, items, or performances.

Project - is temporary in that it has a defined beginning and end in time, and therefore defined scope and resources.

Proprioception - the ability to sense the position and location and orientation and movement of the body and its parts.

RPM - Revolutions per minute is a measure of the frequency of a rotation. It annotates the number of turns completed in one minute around a fixed axis. It is used as a measure of rotational speed of a mechanical component.

Speed - can be thought of as the rate at which an object covers distance. A fast-moving object has a high speed and covers a relatively large distance in a short amount of time.

Strength - is the ability to create muscular tension.

Ventilatory Threshold - it's that intensity of exercise above which your breathing becomes labored and you feel you just can't draw in as much air as your body wants.

VO2 Max – is the maximum capacity of an individual's body to transport and use oxygen during incremental exercise, which reflects the physical fitness of the individual.

Watt - the average human generates around 100 watts in an average day. Depending on the person's activity, weight, and metabolism, a person's power can be slightly higher or lower. Strictly speaking, a watt is a measure of power per unit time (1 joule per second, to be exact). This can contribute to your cycling training because the objective nature of watt-based training gives you much more precision than either heart rate or perceived exertion since it is a measurement of the workload you've done independent from speed, winds, hills and all the other variables that can change how difficult you perceived a ride to be.

Wingate Test - is an anaerobic test, most often performed on a cycle ergometer, that is used to measure peak anaerobic power, as well as anaerobic capacity.

Index

Aero bars, 30
asphalt, 127
cadence, 54
Chainrings, 24
Cogs, 24
contraction, 98
Density, 121
Diet, 117
drills, 88
equipment, 22
fibers, 71
FTP, 49
Functional, 92
Gearing, 27
Glycogen, 62
Hypoxia, 56
Interval, 73
Metabolic, 64
motorcycle, 86
Nutrition, 116
omnium, 14

Oxidation, 55
oxygen, 63
P90X, 101
Periodization, 6
Physical Fitness, 36
Plyometrics, 8
power, 38
preparation, 8
pressure, 121
program, 4
project, 4
resistance, 91
Strength, 8
Supplements, 111
Tabata, 94
taper, 93
test, 47
Tiemeyer, 25
time trial, 11
watts, 46

Printed in Great Britain
by Amazon.co.uk, Ltd.,
Marston Gate.